Life and Death
and the
Things in Between

Pierre Richard Arty, M.D.

Illustrated by
Vince Kekoa Hubbard

ISBN 978-1-63525-914-8 (Paperback)
ISBN 978-1-63525-915-5 (Digital)

Christian Faith Publishing, Inc.
296 Chestnut Street
Meadville, PA 16335
www.christianfaithpublishing.com

Illustrated by Vince Kekoa Hubbard

Printed in the United States of America

Contents

Your Presence

My fearful heart calms as I enter your presence
My spirit awakens refreshed, and it dances
Whatever may come, I know I'll be fine
I have strength for today, to breathe one more time

Only in Your presence am I truly alive
You are my river of life where I blossom and thrive

As the flowers in winter await the spring
My anguished soul slowly rises to sing
Your smile shines on me with radiant favor
I'm in the arms of my Lord, my King, and my Savior

Only in your presence am I truly alive
You are my river of life where I blossom and thrive

Pierre Richard Arty

Inspiration from Psalm 1

I have had the privilege to meet Dr. Pierre Arty as he was a psychiatric resident at Downstate Medical Center. At our first encounter it was obvious that a certain affinity existed between us, perhaps because we are both Haitians who migrated to the United States, although I have always professed that a free man should never let himself get trapped by race or nationality; otherwise he may lose the so precious privilege of freedom. Therefore my evaluation of trainees was always based on their own merits.

As a resident, Dr. Arty demonstrated an acute sense of duty and responsibility in the accomplishment of his daily assignments. But above all, he was a man of sincerity. I have kept that impression of him since I interviewed him, as he was seeking acceptance in the psychiatric residency program at SUNY Downstate Medical Center. I still remember writing in my evaluation that he was socially conscious. Therefore I highly recommended him.

Time has passed and Dr. Arty, who years ago was a young trainee, has gained both professional experience and maturity. His humanistic convictions have led him to help his patients in their times of distress. He has witnessed suffering and death in his own family. Recently his expertise has been sought as far as Malawi. The publication of this book is a new proof of Dr. Arty's determination to share his rich experience with other human beings. There is no doubt that the readers will see this book as an invitation to remain compassionate and courageous in the worst times of adversity.

E.F. Thébaud. M.D.
Clinical Assistant Professor of Psychiatry
SUNY Downstate Medical Center

Dr. Arty's stories are told with compassion, honesty, and heart, sharing with his readers his raw moments of questioning faith while he continues to draw upon that faith and the love he feels for those who love him in return. These are stories of the mentally ill and the disenfranchised, of immigrants and the down and out—stories of life and death, faith, hope, and love. They are stories that touch our hearts with their humanity and their reflection of the human condition from the very specific and kind perspective of a physician, a therapist, a son, a grandson, and a friend.

—T. L. Max McMillen, ELS, Editor-in-Chief, *Leaflet*, a medical literary and visual arts magazine, and Senior Editor, *The Permanente Journal*

In his series of short stories adapted from his personal experience or that of his patients, Pierre vividly weaves an intricate web of each character's story. His depiction of each story is more enthralling than the other, and is written in his distinctive style which is thoughtful and candid. The reader is taken on a heartfelt ride as Pierre explores themes of loss, love, friendship, and hope. This book of short stories will entertain, educate, and take you on an emotional journey.

—Mary Pender Greene, LCSW-R, Psychotherapist/Author, President and CEO of MPG Consulting

Dedication

To the memory of my mother Sylvia Laroche Arty. More than
anyone else, you have contributed to the man I am today.
You have and always will be my source of encouragement, strength,
and unflinching love. You are the most resilient person I know.

To the memory of my sister Carline Arty who patiently listened
to all of my proposed projects and plans throughout the years.
You are the bravest person I ever met.
Your steadfast belief in me means more
to me than you will ever know.

Acknowledgements

The stories in this book span over 20 years. I am grateful to each patient I have had the pleasure of meeting and treating, from my first years as a medical intern to this moment as a practicing Psychiatrist. My patients have shared their emotional lives with me and I am humbled and grateful for the honor that comes with being a person's doctor. They have taught me much about what it means to be a doctor.

It is my hope that many will find comfort in these stories, knowing that "weeping may endure for a night, but joy comes in the morning." Psalm 30:5.

I would like to thank my family, friends, colleagues, teachers such as Dr. E.F. Thébaud and pastors who have provided me with emotional, psychological and spiritual support throughout the years. Special mention goes out to Mr. Reginald Black, my High School English teacher who continues to encourage me to write well.

A special thanks to my wife Wendy who sees what is the very best inside me. She pushes me beyond my own self-imposed boundaries and makes me a better man. I wish Sylvia could have met you.

To my *Charismatic Adult*, father figure and friend Mr. Claude Jean-Pierre, I don't have the words to write my appreciation for you and all that you have contributed to my life. I will start by saying thank you.

And to my father, Mr. Gontran Arty, who taught me much about the importance of prayer and what it is to be actively kind and considerate to others. Your spirit flows through these stories.

Above all else, I thank God who has blessed me with the breath of life, the gift of creativity and all that I have experienced, both the beautiful and the perceived ugly.

God's ways are indeed perfect.

Foreword

I first met Dr. Pierre Arty in the middle of a crowded room of people. "Come here. I want you to meet a Christian psychiatrist," a mutual friend said to me. It was at a missions ministry meeting in a large church in Brooklyn.

We both were interested in reaching out to provide both medical and spiritual care to the poor and neglected in faraway lands around the world. Being a Christian psychiatrist myself, I was eager to meet him. Both in the secular field of psychiatry and in the conservative church, "Christian psychiatrist" is often seen as an oxymoron.

We were introduced, and an immediate connection was made. My very first words were spoken with assumed familiarity, "You understand, don't you?" I said, to which he replied with a knowing smile, "Yes." Here was a Jewish psychiatrist meeting a Haitian psychiatrist in a room filled with others from almost every background—blacks from African nations; the many islands of the Caribbean and the States; orientals from China, Korea, Vietnam, and Japan; Hispanics; Arabs; and Anglos—all together with a common belief and common goals. The heterogeneity was typical of Brooklyn, but the camaraderie was not. It was very special.

Pierre and I each went on more than a few medical teams to the Middle East, Haiti, Africa, India, Cambodia, the Philippines, and Guyana—some together and others separately. I remember when we were sleeping near each other in a room of fellow short-term missionaries and my mosquito netting fell over onto him in his bed. What a trip that was, waking up in the middle of the night, laughing at the unique circumstances in which we found ourselves. I also remember attending his wedding to his beautiful soul mate. What a privilege to know them both.

Pierre and I share many things in common. We both trained in internal medicine before going into psychiatry. We both come from immigrant families that have had to adapt to a foreign culture in a strange new land, making the leap from humble peasant backgrounds to (hopefully equally humble) highly trained professionals— boundary crossers with a sensitivity and awareness of much that others take for granted or don't even notice.

In this book of short stories, Dr. Arty writes often as in a private diary. Emotions, raw and intense, are equally expressed along with detailed factual accounts of both very personal as well as professional experiences. He is a keen observer who is able to articulate with clarity and artistic creativity.

Above all, he is real, transparent, and honest. The stories are ones to which we can all relate. Some invite us into the world of medicine and mental health and show the human, the personal, the relational in what would otherwise be seen as an environment of the mechanical and instrumental. Below the surface, however, are the universal feelings of despair, terror, and rage that we all must conquer so we can arrive at true hope, peace, and joy.

Dr. Arty wants to share with others in and beyond his present spheres of influence. To his leadership in his religious and professional communities and his accomplishments as a playwright, he now adds his talent as a writer of short stories.

He models what we all need to increasingly embrace. See if you don't agree as you enter into his world, and he, in turn, enters into yours.

Dr. Irving S. Wiesner, MD
Author of *Tools from Psychiatry for the Journey of Faith*

TapTap

He is driving on Church Avenue in the East Flatbush section of Brooklyn, New York, during the busiest time of the day. It is late afternoon, rush hour to millions of Brooklynites heading home after a long day's work. He is one of several TapTap drivers, often-uninsured individuals who have taken upon themselves the responsibility to answer the need for a quick—and hopefully safe—transportation for the hundreds of people trying to get home after exiting from various subway stations. They are heading to a place where the inhabitants look like they do, speak the same language, cook and eat food that reaffirms who they are after being with outsiders for most of their day. These days, the inhabitants are mostly West Indian, coming from various Caribbean islands such as Haiti, Trinidad, Jamaica, St. Lucia, and Barbados. They even hail from places in Central America and South America, such as Panama and Guyana, respectively. But it wasn't always like this.

Immigrants made up of Jews and Italians populated this area during the post-World War II period. In the 1960s, African Americans were the dominant group. Now these inhabitants, made up of mostly those from the Caribbean, are struggling to get home to be with their families.

He also knows that the buses that carry them home never arrive promptly. And even if they do, they are often overcrowded with strangers standing closer to one another than they would like to be, especially after a long day's work.

With these thoughts in mind, he is encouraged by the fact that he is performing a very important function. He knows that he does not have the license to do this, and the police frequently stop his fellow TapTap drivers after their cars are filled with passengers. But no amount of summonses has been able to stop these drivers from fulfilling their roles. Besides, it was good money. Why should the city make that money?

He has two children and a wife whom he left almost four years ago in Cap-Haitien, a large city in the north coast of Haiti. He works hard so that he can save enough money to bring them to America. The pictures of his children, a girl six and the boy seven, are taped onto the dashboard of his car. He thinks of them throughout the day, but especially at night as he tries to sleep in the little apartment on Beverly Road that he shares with several of his cousins from Trou-Du-Nord, a town northeast of Cap-Haitien.

The furniture in his room includes a small television set where he watches a Haitian news station, a radio, and a rectangular table where he keeps an old Bible, forever opened to Psalm 23. In the shoebox next to the Bible is a photograph of his parents. A framed picture of his wife and children is placed next to his mattress. In the closet is the suit that he wears every Sunday to attend the Catholic mass, a black pair of shoes, and one of two pairs of jeans that he owns. He is wearing the other pair, along with some sneakers—Karochu, he calls them—that he had bought from a 99¢ store. Along with a few shirts and some undergarments, those were the only clothes that he allowed himself to buy since he is so focused on sending every cent to his family. On weekends, he works as a waiter in a Haitian restaurant in Queens.

A few short blocks away on Nostrand Avenue is the barbershop he frequents, even when he doesn't have the need for a haircut. It is there that he is able to get the news behind the news from the experts on Haitian politics, the local patrons. His only major expense occurred last month when he paid for a dental extraction after experiencing intolerable pain from an impacted wisdom tooth. Since he didn't have any insurance to pay the dentist, he left with the understanding that he would make occasional payments until his bill was fully paid.

At night, when the mice allow him to sleep, he dreams of his *Haiti Cherie*, his darling Haiti. As he dreams, he feels the soothing sensations of her gentle breezes on his face and smells the aroma of fried fish being cooked on the white sandy beaches bound by her beautiful clear blue sea. But he is only to be awakened in the early hours of the morning, needing to urinate and realizing that he is in a small room, alone in a foreign land wrestling with a strange language. The dream often evaporates before the taste of the salty fish leaves his mouth. Recently, he has been waking up more often than usual by the presence of an emptiness in his chest and tears under his eyelids. It is as if a hole was left in his chest where his heart should be.

More than once while lying on the mattress that was placed on the floor for him to sleep, he found himself wondering if in some way he wasn't experiencing a folly or obsession, in hoping that he could do something more for his family while in New York than if he had stayed *Lacaye*, back home. He wanted to remove them from the dead-end poverty that was the very fabric of their existence.

The generosity of his parents, in-laws, and friends allowed him to collect enough money to leave Haiti for America, a country known for its opportunities. He left with tears in his eyes and a promise on his lips to reunite his family. On many nights while lying on his mattress, awake with his eyes closed, the whisper of a thought kept resonating inside his mind—that maybe he made a mistake.

In New York, he managed to get a driver's license and learned the route of the B35 bus all along Church Avenue, even beyond Utica Avenue, where most of the people from the Caribbean live. Although the car he is driving is not his own, he has an agreement with the owner to return the car with a full tank of gas and a fifty-dollar bill upon completion of each of his regular evening tours. After a couple of months, he even learned how to detect the undercover police cruisers and would purposefully avoid picking up passengers when he saw them from a distance. He grew up hearing the many stories of people who had "disappeared" while in the custody of the Haitian secret police, the *Macoutes*, and he had no desire to disappear in America in the hands of these uniformed white men with his family's future at stake. There was also word out on the streets that the mayor, the magistrate of the land, someone named Giuliani, wasn't one to play with. He had already heard of what had happened to one unfortunate Haitian man named Louima who wound up in the hands of the police one night. He knew that he was taking a chance in doing what he did, but he couldn't pass up this opportunity. The need was there, and so there he was.

This afternoon, he seems to be having a bit more difficulty picking up passengers. Too often, some other TapTap driver is able to rush ahead of him and quickly pick up a potential passenger. *This is not good*, he thinks. If he doesn't begin to make some progress soon, he won't be able to return the car with the fifty-dollar borrowing fee.

His right palm slams on the car horn several times. Feeling frustrated, he notices an odor that is slowly surrounding him like a fog on a warm summer night. At first, it is just a hint, the kind he often makes a mental note of as he drives pass the landfill on the Belt Parkway near Starrett City, but quickly forgets. As he continues to drive, the odor appears to be getting worse, filling up every area of his car. He looks outside at the pedestrians to see if anyone notices this pungent smell, but people seem to be occupied with their own personal matters. He decides to stop the car and check the backseat to see if any passengers had accidentally left some food in the back. After getting out of the car and making his inspection, he finds nothing out of the ordinary in the back. Getting out of the car doesn't help either. The horrible odor is all around him, and it is getting stronger. He gets back into the driver's seat wondering if a sewer cover was left open somewhere near. And again, another TapTap driver passes him to pick up a passenger that he had visually claimed as his from half a block away. *Tonnere foutre!* "Damn!" he hears himself shout as his right fist punches the car horn.

As he is driving and now actively looking for potential passengers, he catches the reflection of his face in the rearview mirror. He is actively perspiring, and the look of anger is clear in his eyes. He tells himself that he has to calm down. As he takes another look at his face, trying to make it look calm, he notices his mouth, and his mind takes him back to several weeks ago when he had visited the dentist. Slowly, the wall of a mental dam begins to crack. For the first time in his life, he seriously entertains a thought that a few days ago would not have made any sense, would even be comical, but now seems to explain everything: *Could it be that…maybe …no. That kind of thing can't… Yes! Of course! It's my mouth…there's something wrong with my mouth…my breath.*

The thought that his breath is the cause of this horrible stench that is getting progressively worse begins to eat at his mind, transforming it, hijacking and carrying it away to a dark and frightening place. Suddenly, the mental dam breaks, and he sees the world differently, as if for the first time. The events of the past several hours take on a new meaning. *That's why I haven't gotten any passengers today*, he reasons to himself. It all makes sense. It is now perfectly clear to him that these people know what is going on, but they are making believe that they don't. *Why haven't I noticed that before?* he wonders.

Somewhere in his mind, a remnant of rationalization tries to reason with him while he feels his blood pressure rising to his head, punching at his temples. *These thoughts can't be real*, he begins to think. *There must be another reason for this odor*, he says to himself. His ears begin to hurt from the vibrations of his heartbeat pounding in his head, sounding louder than Haitian drums in the night. He begins to wonder if someone might have even placed a voodoo curse on him. As he continues to struggle with his inner demons, he is so lost in his thoughts that he doesn't notice the light at the intersection that has just turned red. He is barely able to stop in time.

While impatiently waiting at the light, he notices one of the other TapTap drivers in the opposite lane picking up passengers. As he is looking at the driver, his happenstance look turns into a wide-eyed gaze as the man, who is busy watching the car in front of him, begins to momentarily scratch his nose with the tip of his pointer finger. That is all the evidence that he needs to allow the last vestiges of his sanity to burst behind a flood of lunacy. By that man's incidental nose scratching, he knows that the world is aware that the horrible odor is coming from him. As his breathing becomes louder, he is certain that it is only a matter of time before the police apprehend him for this unforgivable crime and cause him to disappear, never to see his family or country again. The possibility of disappearing in a foreign country without anyone knowing what happened was worse than the language barrier that held him at a distance from everyone but fellow Haitians. *No*, he thinks, *it can't end this way*.

When the light turns green, he presses hard on the gas, making the tires scream, causing pedestrians to look his way. He speeds off and quickly cuts into the opposite lane in order to pass the car ahead of him. He gets back into his lane as soon as he is able to and continues to drive the car wildly, crossing an intersection. He continues with this brazen driving into the opposite lane every now and then, catching the attention of passersby. "You crazy?" he hears them yell at him.

"Madman…you gonna kill somebody," someone else screams.

Coming to Nostrand Avenue, he sees the light going from yellow to red, and he accelerates even more, crossing the intersection just as the light changes to red. His heart is racing now, and his hands begin to tremble. He can feel his palms becoming sweaty, soaking the steering wheel with moisture. He is constantly looking at his rearview mirror, searching for anyone who may be following him. He is now heading toward the next intersection at New York Avenue, and he notices the pictures of his children taped to the dashboard. *These are the reasons I came to this country*, he thinks. *This is why I can't disappear. Ede m Bondye…mwen fatige avek lavi sa a.* "God help me, I'm tired of this life," he cries out as tears begin to make their way down his dark-brown cheeks.

He begins to sob almost uncontrollably behind the wheel of the car while driving faster than he should on a city road. Suddenly, in the darkness of his mind, a memory begins to shine some light. He remembers the hospital in the neighborhood that is known even in Haiti. He remembers stories of how people would come right off the airplane from John F. Kennedy Airport, head directly to Kings County Hospital, and receive treatment for their illnesses. He had also heard the patrons at the barbershop joke about people who were treated at the "G" building, where "moun fou," crazy people, are kept. *Maybe I am losing my mind*, he thinks.

Reaching Albany and Church Avenue, he quickly makes a left turn, heading for where he heard this "G" building was located. The tears flow freely now, and he barely recognizes the man that occasionally glances back at him in the rearview mirror. At Clarkson and Albany Avenues, he takes the red light, nearly colliding with a woman in a black Volvo. She curses at him as he speeds off, only to stop at the end of the block where a parking space is waiting for him.

After parking the car and placing the keys in his pocket, he runs across Albany Avenue into the entrance of the Psychiatric Emergency Room. He then pushes the doors open and heads straight for the first person he sees in white hospital scrubs. He grabs the nurse forcefully by the arm and frantically begins to yell, "Help me. Help me," while crying uncontrollably and frightening her. By this time, two security officers who are posted at the entrance of the emergency room quickly approach this apparently dangerous intruder. He notices their approach and screams out, "*Anmwe*, help!" Thinking that these officers are the New York City police, he tries to evade them in a small and confined emergency room, all the while screaming, "*Anmwe...Anmwe!*" This only attracts more uniformed officers into the now established melee. As they try to talk to him, he becomes more agitated. Even if they were able to speak his language, it would have been futile. At this point, he believes that they are all a part of a conspiracy to kidnap him, and his family will never hear from him again. He makes a feeble attempt to fight off the officers, which only results in being restrained and carried into a room, away from everyone. Now in this confined place, he continues to cry loudly in Creole, asking God for forgiveness for many imagined sins.

Later, he is found on his knees in a pool of tears when a Haitian psychiatrist eventually comes to speak to him. He is inconsolable and wishes only to end his life since he is a failure and he believes the world knows it. The odor from his mouth is evidence of that. He agrees to let the doctor give him some medication more out of respect than with a hope that it will make a difference in his outcome. The doctor says that the medication is for his nerves, and soon he feels the penetration of a small needle in his right shoulder. In a few moments, he begins to feel groggy, then sleepy. His last thoughts before falling asleep are that of his wife and children, who are depending on him to send money home.

Through My Mother's Eyes

T his is a story about my mother, Sylvia, and a story about a devastating stroke that changed everything. But before I tell you more about the stroke, I need to tell you a little about her.

My mother was born in Haiti, in a large city called Cap-Haitien, known as "Au Cap" to most Haitians. It is a city known for its busy and colorful marketplaces or "marchés," where women from the surrounding towns come to engage in commerce while gracefully balancing merchandise on their heads. Situated in the northern part of Haiti, I have heard it said that most of the revolutionaries came from there, and judging from my mother's volatile temper and drive, I believe that to be true. I also believe the major influence in her life was her father, René Laroche, my grandfather.

René was a man of meticulous idiosyncrasies. These included taking showers with very cold water and always sitting at the dinner table formally, even if just to eat a sandwich. It was a rare thing to find him walking under the hot Haitian sun without wearing a crisp white shirt and tie.

René stressed that education was the key to living in a civilized world, and this belief in the power of education was something my mother passed on to me. It is our cable, our umbilical cord between generations. She raised me to believe that education is the road to success, the way for a black man to make a mark in a white man's world. With this value system as a background, she gave me my first identity in this world.

My mother immigrated to the United States in 1968, leaving my father, younger sister Carline, and I to rejoin her a year later in New York City. Like most immigrants from the Caribbean, she came to the States in search of a better life for herself and her family.

We lived in a one-bedroom apartment on Empire Boulevard in the East Flatbush section of Brooklyn. I remember happy times as a child in that apartment, when she would hold me tight and try to teach me to dance to the traditional music of Haitian parties, *Compas Direct*. The more I fussed and tried to get away, the tighter she held on to me, until I relented and learned to dance. Like most childhoods, if the whole truth were to be told, it would reveal events that were far from ideal. Strife, arguments, and anger filled our apartment more times than I care to remember, but I prefer to remember the good times.

There were times during my years in school when she actively demonstrated how much she wanted me to succeed.

During my high school years, I remember her staying up with me until the early hours of the morning, typing a paper for me that was due that day. When a typing mistake occurred, she had to get a bottle of Wite-Out and wait until the white liquid dried on the typing paper before she could begin typing again. This typing and stopping to make corrections went on throughout the night until eventually I would fall asleep to the comforting tap of the typewriter keys, letting me know that I wasn't alone.

During medical school, I often felt so overwhelmed by the course work that I didn't even know where to begin studying. The nights before the biochemistry exams were the worst. On several occasions, after staying up most of the night studying, I would become anxious and feel as if I couldn't remember anything that I had studied. Thoughts of failure would enter my mind; and it was only my mother's voice—or her silent yet reassuring presence at the other end of the phone at two, three, or four in the morning—that was able to chase those thoughts away and still my anxious heart.

Today, we are at a Brooklyn rehabilitation hospital, in a room with large windows facing the entrance. Well-manicured hedges greet visitors by spelling out the word *Welcome* before they enter the main doors of the facility. I look in those familiar brown eyes and see a prisoner, screaming to get out but not able to make a sound. Her eyebrows come together and move upward in a look of sadness and discomfort. The wrinkles on her forehead express that familiar look, daring me to help her. I find it hard to believe that this is my mother, the woman who bore me and raised me, who may know me better than I know myself, staring at me like a helpless frightened child.

I have to find out what the source of her discomfort is before she crosses the threshold from discomfort to pain. *What could it be?* I wonder. *Is it the way she's sitting in the wheelchair? Should I change her position? Has she been sitting too long? Does she have a headache or cramp and need to be placed back in bed? Oh God...how I hate that look...that language spoken through the eyes that I can never seem to understand. I begin searching frantically, for what those eyes are saying.*

Two years earlier, at fifty-eight years of age, my mother had a severe stroke in the left side of her brain, rendering her forever unable to speak her thoughts. Moreover, it meant that her world was changed forever. She became a different person overnight. That incredibly functional woman who used to walk across the Brooklyn Bridge in the afternoons for exercise, the woman who used to prepare a consoling cup of tea for me at five o'clock in the morning after I got home from a strenuous night on call at the hospital... that woman was undeniably gone. She was replaced by a broken shell with my mother's spirit entombed inside. This was Sylvia's first death. Years later, I would come to appreciate how much of Pierre had also died that day.

Soon after the stroke, she spent several days in a coma and was later placed on a respirator. Unfortunately, when the effort was made to have her breathe on her own, it became difficult, and she developed complications.

She consequently underwent a tracheotomy and tube placement to make her more comfortable as the respirator continued to breathe for her. Several weeks later, when she came out of her coma, an attempt was made to remove the tube; but she nearly aspirated on her own sputum. She was eventually weaned off the respirator, but the tracheotomy tube, otherwise known as a "trach," stayed.

In the room, an overhead television is showing her favorite performer, Neil Diamond, at a concert singing, "Sweet Caroline... good times never seemed so good." Her mouth opens to say something, and what her mouth cannot say, her left hand goes on to elaborate. She shakes her left hand in front of my face, and I hear the heavy breathing from her opened trach tube, which decorates her smooth neckline like a medallion on a necklace. I touch her right arm to make sure that the brace is not too tight, and the left hand vehemently begins to move up and down. "I'm doing something wrong," I say to myself, beginning to feel frustrated. She doesn't look at what I'm doing on the right side but winces as I move the right arm. I go on to explore her right thigh and knee. I do this methodically, not wanting to miss anything.

In addition to her speech deficit, Sylvia's right side is paralyzed. This paralysis includes the lower right half of her beautiful face and results in a crooked smile whenever she greets anyone. The right hand is useless, and the right leg is a lesson in frustration. The rehabilitation team assigned to her works feverishly at trying to prevent the contracture that is slowly compromising the extension of the knee. She already needs a brace for her right hand as contractures are spreading along the length of her fingers like a stubborn rash. It all seems like a futile fight against the inevitable.

In the first months after her stroke, I was asked to consent to the placement of a tube into her stomach in order to have her fed directly. Up until that time, her nutrition came through the combination of both nasogastric and intravenous tubes because her doctors and I were not sure if she was yet able to swallow. Unfortunately, these sources of feeding were not providing sufficient calories.

I remember looking at my mother with the eyes of both a doctor and a son. I saw a woman lying in a hospital bed with an intravenous tube in her left arm, another tube sticking out of her nose and a catheter protruding from her bladder. I dreaded the thought of another tube in her body. *Another invasion of her body and another risk for infection*, I thought.

"Listen, let me work with her for a week…If she is not able to swallow by that time, I'll agree to the tube," was my response to the staff. As the doctors turned to leave, I whispered a prayer, "Lord, I'm going to need your help."

As if in answer, it occurred to me to begin feeding her with soft food like ice cream or yogurt. I immediately went out, bought some yogurt, and, with a small spoon, began trying to feed her. "Mommy, you have to learn to eat and swallow again," I said to her. With a nod, she seemed to understand."

I began by giving her small mouthfuls and, with great anticipation, waited to see if she would cough or swallow. She looked directly into my eyes and allowed the spoon to come to her lips. Slowly, her jaw began to move. I wasn't sure if she swallowed or not, but she did not choke. Mercifully, she did not choke. I felt the air slowly come out of my chest while her eyes were fixed on mine.

After checking her mouth for any trace of the yogurt, I gave her another spoonful, ready to act if she should show any signs of trouble. Surprisingly, she opened her mouth automatically as if she had never stopped eating and invited the spoon in. I watched with anxious excitement as she closed her lips against the spoon to hide the yogurt in her mouth. She kept on looking at me with those childlike brown eyes that seemed to be asking, "Am I doing this right? Is this what I should be doing?"

Next, we tried ice cream, and she went after the ice cream with a purpose, letting the remnants drip down the corners of her mouth. "That's it...I knew you could do it!" I said. We continued this diet of yogurt and ice cream while she was still receiving intravenous supplements.

Sometime during the course of these exercises, she had removed the nasogastric tube from her nose. I guess she decided that she no longer needed it.

After a week, the staff trusted me enough to try feeding my mother mashed potatoes. We started from the beginning, once again letting her tongue taste the mashed potatoes and later allowing her to swallow a small portion of what was on the spoon. With each mouthful that she swallowed, I felt more and more encouraged.

Later, when we gained more confidence in her ability to swallow, friends and family would bring other dishes for her to eat. My sister Carline would meticulously feed her while her eyes went from the spoon to our faces and then to the television, always glancing to the left. She especially enjoyed a fish soup brought by our family friend Carmen P. She never did have to have the stomach tube placed.

Continuing my examination, I check the brace placed on her right leg and heel pad protecting her right foot. As I look at her foot, I remember the times my sister Carline came, sat on the chair placed at the foot of the hospital bed, and used her cosmetology skills to give my mother a pedicure. Entering the room during those times, my mother would greet me with her smile. That crooked smile would greet visitors as they entered the room, followed by those bright eyes, inviting them in.

While I'm examining her foot, her left hand continues to shake, with the pointer finger waving in the air. The pinky, ring, and middle fingers of the left hand are already partially contracted. It makes the left hand always look as if it is pointing to something even when she is just waving good-bye. I am still at a loss as to what could be the source of her discomfort. I move on to examine the left side of her body, which should not be the source of any pain or discomfort. After all, she has a great degree of mobility on that left side. I bend down to examine the nicely manicured left hand, but she pulls away from me with a strength and rudeness that surprises me. I understand that she has grown impatient with my efforts. More than impatient, she is angry.

Sylvia had always been short-tempered, and my impression is that her stroke opened a floodgate in that area of her emotional life. I would often see the frustration in her face when she was trying to communicate a thought, and no one was able to grasp the meaning. It was like chasing shadows. We were consequently forced to look deeper into her eyes for the woman that once was and try to decipher her new language. Many times after these clumsy efforts at communication, she would wave her left hand as if to say, "Forget it," and angrily focus on the television, ignoring all else.

I leave her hand alone and turn my attention to her left thigh and foot. I don't seem to be getting any closer to whatever is disturbing her. I examine the thigh and go to massage her muscles. She pushes me away with that left hand, clearly telling me, "That's not what's bothering me!"

"Mommy, *map essaye aide ou*," I say in Creole, which means, "I'm trying to help you." But my words fall on deaf ears. She is now absorbed in her pain and just wants relief. I am supposed to provide her with that relief, but I don't know how. She is fighting me. She has had enough of this blind man bumping into fragile objects. She rejects any further intervention on my part and looks up at Neil Diamond, who is singing another song to her.

As for me, I stand up exasperated. Droplets of sweat cover my forehead, and an emotional exhaustion seeps deep into my soul.

We are both frustrated at the other's limitations, and words are not needed at this point; they would just get in the way. She is obviously frustrated at her newfound limitations, along with my general incompetence, and looks up to hold on to one comforting pleasure of her past life—the songs of her favorite performer. I'm angry at life's apparent unfairness and my own inability to pierce this hellish communication barrier. I feel frustrated with what I see as a lack of appreciation on her part for my efforts to help her. But I also wonder what else lies behind those bright eyes staring at the television.

What would she say to me if she could? A year ago, those same eyes had opened wide as she looked at me from her hospital bed as if I had suddenly grown a tail when I shared with her my plans to begin a residency in psychiatry. Although at the time I had not yet begun my psychiatric training, I didn't need any such training to clearly understand what she was not able to say. Today, as a first-year psychiatric resident, I am lost. *Does she see herself through my eyes? Is this why she is now refusing to look at me? If so, is she rejecting my help? Or possibly, is it some aspect of her? Does she meditate on precious hopes and dreams that will never be or on memories of a prior life?*

Even now as I take a moment to contemplate these questions and reflect on my own fleeting hopes for her full recovery, her face begins to grimace in pain, and she looks at me again, this time with tears that make her eyes glisten. I swear I can almost hear her shout, "Help me!" with the ears of my heart. I bend down again, but the only thing remaining is her left foot. I suddenly notice the foot shaking up and down, not with a lot of power, but definitely shaking. *Was it shaking before?* I wonder. *Did I just notice that?* Since this was her functional or "good" foot, she wears a sneaker that nicely matches her warm-up clothes. She lets me touch it.

I hold her ankle with my left hand and remove her sneaker from her foot with my right hand. I hear the familiar sound of her exhalation from the opening of her trach tube and look up to see that crooked smile of hers. She is smiling and looking down at me with those beautiful bright brown eyes. It is then that I realize that her sneaker laces had been tied too tightly, and this is the cause of her distress. *Such a simple thing.*

We stare at one another, and our eyes speak with perfect understanding. She touches my chin with her left pointer finger, gently lifts my face up to her lips, and kisses my cheek. I laugh and cry at the same time.

Petals and Thorns

I've been driving around this cemetery for the last twenty minutes looking for my mother's grave, and I feel frustrated. I'm angry with myself because my mother's longtime confidant, Claude, gave me clear instructions on how to get to the gravesite, and I still can't find it. I remember the last time that I was here, over a year ago, I could see a subway station from where the plaque marking my mother's gravesite rested on the cemetery ground. But it seems I've lost my bearings. *It must be the rain*, I reason with myself. I haven't visited my mother's grave in more than a year, and I chose a rainy day to come out to a muddy cemetery to visit. What am I out here for anyway? As far as I'm concerned, she's gone, and the grave is just a marker of her remains.

But today is the first Mother's Day without Sylvia, and I really want to give her these roses. I chose the "Fire and Ice" roses that I knew she loved while she was alive. They are hybrids, a cross between red and white roses that develop dark red petals in the interior with a beautiful white exterior. My mother always loved receiving flowers from me, and there is no one else that I would rather give flowers to today. I came here to say happy Mother's Day, and I can't find her gravesite.

All the gravesites at this cemetery look the same to me. Each one is assigned a plaque which is placed on the burial site of the deceased. Now if only I could find Sylvia's burial site.

A little more than a year ago, I was standing in this cemetery, at the edge of the dark hole that would swallow my mother's coffin. The priest had just finished offering his last prayers; and I was with my sister, father, and aunts Marijo and Ginette, in the first row of people lining up to throw roses in the grave. I let the rose drop from my hand, unconsciously perhaps, symbolizing either a last gesture of love or a letting go of the dead. I watched it fall slowly onto the cover of the coffin without a sound. Moments later, other roses were thrown from behind me, hiding the cover of the casket with a blanket of red petals and thorns. I stepped back to allow others to say their good-byes, while Claude began to take pictures of the casket.

It was a cold morning in early February, and it began to snow. The trees lining the cemetery grounds looked naked with their bare thin branches extending upward toward the heavens, as if offering supplications to the Creator. The sky was cloudy, and I couldn't detect any birds on the tree branches or in the sky. A chill in the air bit deep into my soul. The longer I stayed at the gravesite, the more I felt my soul being torn piece by piece. People spoke to one another, their breaths forming clouds of mist that lingered after the words were gone.

The cemetery workers started shoveling dirt into the grave, and many of the mourners returned to the warmth of their cars. I stayed a little longer, watching the backhoe drop cold hard dirt onto my mother's casket.

Today feels much like that cold February morning. I had thought of inviting a friend to come with me, but I wasn't sure how I would have reacted, so I decided to go alone. Being alone gave me some time to think about Sylvia and the period surrounding her death. I remembered the night I left my mother's hospital room after a visit.

She was sitting in her wheelchair, watching television with Claude. I wanted to get home early to get a good night's sleep since I knew I would be on call the next day. It was a cool January night, and Sylvia had passed the day well, smiling at guests, giving no indication of pain or discomfort. For the past couple of months, she had appeared more and more serene in her demeanor. She emanated an inner peace that contrasted with the restlessness surrounding her during the first years of her stroke—her first death. Her peace was contagious and affected everyone around her. Her smile was captivating and made you wonder how she managed to maintain it with all of her recent physical limitations. I knew she was placed on an antidepressant, but that didn't really explain it—antidepressants are not "happy pills." They just help one cope with depression so that one sees the glass as half full rather than half empty. They don't provide joy.

In a way only she and her Maker understood, they seemed to have come to a mutual agreement beyond anyone else's understanding and now walked together, arm in arm. Having lost the capacity for speech, and as a prisoner in her own mind, she had no one else to talk to. It was three long years of speaking to her Creator in whatever form that communication took. But she loved to receive guests, especially children and strangers. Her eyes would light up when a child visited, and it seemed at times that her loved ones had a harder time dealing with her stroke than she did. She made it feel good to visit her.

I got up from my chair, put on my coat, walked over to my mother, bent, and kissed her on the cheek. She looked at me and smiled. As I left the room, I said, "Good-bye, Mommy…I'll see you tomorrow, all right? I'll be working close by, so I'll stop in."

She mouthed something to me, and I understood it to mean, "Get home safe. I'll see you tomorrow." Claude and I shook hands, and as I walked toward the elevator, I made an effort not to think about how my mother handled the nights.

Her aphasia had locked her inside herself, inside her mind. I continuously wondered what happened to her in the middle of the night when she woke up thirsty or after a nightmare. How was she consoled when she cried in the early hours of the morning? Was it in these hours that she made peace with her Savior? I even wondered what her thought life must have been like in light of her stroke. Did she think as we do, with words forming goal-directed sentences, or were her thoughts expressed as waves of dark and light emotions? I went home that night feeling tired but somehow encouraged, believing that the worse was behind us.

The next day, while I was driving on the Gowanus Expressway in Brooklyn, several calls activated my beeper in a one-minute span. It seemed that all of a sudden almost everyone close to me, including my father, Gontran, was trying to contact me. Feeling a sense of urgency, I got off the highway, found a public phone, and contacted my father. He told me the hospital had called looking for me and requested that I come quickly. Apparently, my mother was not doing well.

With anxiety as a driving partner, I rushed to the hospital as swiftly as I could. I took the elevator to the floor where my mother was hospitalized. Moving quickly out of the elevator toward my mother's ward, I ran directly into several doctors and nurses crowding outside my mother's room. My mother was being coded. I had walked right into my own mother's cardiac arrest!

By this point in my medical career, I had been involved in and functioned as the code leader in several cardiac arrests. However, never in my most far-fetched fantasies did I ever think that I would be present during my mother's code. I felt an urge to get involved, to do something, even if it was just to hand a pair of gloves to a nurse. It seemed as if the code team was also unsure of what to do with me. They knew I was a doctor and familiar with code situations, but this was an uncomfortable situation for us all. Detecting their nervousness, I walked into an empty hospital room to let the staff carry on with what they had to do without the added stress of seeing me. I continued a prayer I had begun years ago. I prayed for either my mother's life or for God to take her home that very day. Those were the words of my prayer, but my heart was not ready to let her go. It would never be ready.

In the room, I heard the code leader giving orders for medications and the hurried footsteps of staff passing the open doorway. After what seemed like an eternity, the medical resident came into the room to say that my mother was resuscitated and had her tracheotomy tube attached to a ventilator. She was to be transferred to the intensive care unit. No one knew what had caused the cardiac arrest, but her prognosis was not good. That was Sylvia's second death.

The sound of rain lightly tapping against my windshield brings my thoughts to the tortuous hours and days after her cardiac arrest. I drive a little slower now, not wanting to miss any landmarks that will give me a clue to the whereabouts of my mother's gravesite. It is becoming harder to concentrate on my driving as the memory of days of waiting and hoping while my mother was in the ICU comes back to haunt me like a vengeful ghost.

My mother was transferred to the medical wing of the rehabilitation facility to await an ICU bed. I took the opportunity to call my sister Carline and father to let them know what was happening. I left it to them to contact other family members. Approximately twenty minutes later, I was allowed to enter the medical room where she lay. I walked in quietly after being directed to the room by the nurse in charge. The noise of the ventilator that now breathed for my mother spoke to me of her condition. I listened to its mechanical vibrations telling me about the poor prognosis. As my footsteps neared her hospital bed, I realized that I didn't want to look at her face, but I found myself looking, searching for any semblance of the woman I said good night to only a few short hours ago.

Amazingly, her face was already disfigured. Her jaw and lips looked swollen as she lay with her head flat against the pillow. Her eyelids were not fully closed, and I saw dried tear tracks running down the corners of both eyes to her ears. Those inviting eyes were gone, replaced by two swollen sclera that seemed to be pushing against glazed pupils underneath partially closed eyelids. Crusted blood encircled the area around her tracheotomy and painted the corners of her mouth like smudged lipstick. As I stood at her bedside, I remember whispering to her, "Mommy, Mommy," feeling like a small lost child in a large dark forest. There was no answer. Sylvia was gone.

At that moment, what I saw and came to know, my sister somehow knew instinctively. Sometime later, Carline mentioned to me how that very morning, while showering, she somehow knew that our mother had died. She said, "I knew she was dead, but I didn't want to admit it to myself…I felt her spirit passing through me, and I felt her love. It was a warm feeling from my head to my toes. It came and went. I didn't know she loved me like that. I cried in the shower that morning."

By the time other family members came, Sylvia had been transferred to the ICU where for twelve days family and friends visited and prayed. Mostly people stayed outside the unit. Sylvia looked horrible, and it was a painful thing to watch her physically deteriorate so quickly. We continued to pray, and she continued to get worse. My mother developed multiorgan failure, including her kidneys and her blood constituents. She became more and more swollen each day that she received medications and intravenous fluids to help maintain her blood pressure. Eventually, her platelets, which help in coagulation, began to decrease in numbers, and she began to bleed spontaneously from almost every orifice including the corners of her mouth and nostrils. In order to fight against her chronic deterioration, I made it a point each night before leaving the ICU to hold hands and form a circle around Sylvia with whoever had come to visit. We would stand and intercede for a miraculous healing. The healing I hoped for never came.

During the week, almost every subspecialty service of medicine was consulted to give input on my mother's condition, but no one was able to help. The hematology service predictably requested permission to perform a bone marrow biopsy in order to determine the cause of her low platelets. Against my better judgment, I allowed it. It did not affect the prognosis in any way, and it was the last invasive procedure I allowed on my mother's body.

Eventually, there was not much left that was recognizable as Sylvia. Standing next to her hospital bed, I thought about how several years earlier I was able to make a clear decision about how aggressive the care should be for my dying grandmother. But this time around, I held on to hope and allowed this tortuous game of hoping and waiting to continue to a very bitter end. God could do anything, this I didn't doubt. But as the days came and went, his will became more and more clear. Sylvia was gone, and she wasn't coming back. Now we, the family, had to let the body go.

Several days later, I signed the do-not-resuscitate order, indicating that if her heart should stop, no attempt should be made to revive her. I felt incredible disappointment and exhaustion, but I also felt a strong sense of release and acceptance of the situation. I was very much at peace with this decision.

Two days later on January 30, 1997, at approximately 6:45 a.m., I received a phone call from Claude, telling me with a cracked voice that my mother's heart had stopped beating at approximately 6:40 a.m. This was Sylvia's third and final death. Although this phone call was expected, Carline and I still felt the aftershocks of her passing. Later that day, Claude met me in the lobby of the hospital after I had gone to retrieve my mother's belongings. We sat together not saying much, just letting the reality of Sylvia's passing sink in.

I'm beginning to recognize some of the terrain even through my foggy windshield. Thankfully, the rain appears to be lifting, and I think

I see a landmark. There's the entrance to the subway that I had noticed a year ago. Yes, the ground is starting to look more familiar. Unless I'm mistaken, the grave must be in that direction. I park my car where I remember several cars had parked last year and step out, reaching for the small bouquet of flowers in the backseat. I brought two "Fire and Ice" roses for my mother. They represent Carline and me.

I close the car door and head toward where I think the gravesite should be. It is only drizzling now, so I leave my umbrella in the car. I can feel the softness of the ground give in to my weight as I walk on the wet grass. I make an unsuccessful effort to avoid the grassless muddy parts. I walk up a little hill, and I think I should have arrived at the gravesite already, but I can't find it. I pass a number of plaques and read several of their dedications. So far I don't see my mother's plaque. I feel my anxiety, and I'm surprised at my emotional reaction. I'm becoming very annoyed, and I can feel my anger rising. I mean, for the love of God, I can't find her remains! I'm out here trying to avoid walking in mud on a lousy rainy day looking for my mother's grave, and I can't find it!

Suddenly, my anxiety bursts into a powerful awareness of her absence over the past year, and I fear losing her all over again. A cool wind begins to blow the drizzle against my face, and I walk down the hill and head west, not knowing if I am going in the right direction but feeling that I have to keep moving. I remember the last time I saw my mother's body. It was at her wake.

My mother's wake was held for one night, on Friday, February 7, 1997, in the Mill Basin section of Brooklyn. The week before the wake was spent choosing a coffin and the dress that my mother would be buried in. My aunt Ginette provided the dress. The funeral home had several rooms, which were all very neat and inviting. We were given a spacious room due to the fact that we anticipated many people coming to the wake. My mother had helped many people in various ways throughout her life and made countless friends. These individuals, including members from both my parents' families, were expected to attend the only night of the wake.

Her body was kept at the far end of the room in a partially opened casket chosen several days before. The body in the casket looked like my mother, and then again, it didn't. It resembled a bloated caricature of the beautiful woman Sylvia was. The only thing that was natural about it was the hair. Whoever had arranged her hair did a decent job, and the texture was the same as I remembered it. I didn't spend much time near the body. I stayed close to the entrance, greeting both family and friends. My father also stayed near the entrance holding lighthearted and friendly conversation with relatives.

Many family members came. There were several I had not seen for years, and some I didn't even recognize. Childhood friends came to say farewell to a woman who had been a second mother to them. Fellow residents and colleagues from the psychiatric residency program attended, and even the staff of the rehabilitation facility came to say good-bye to the patient they had cared for during these last three difficult years. They, along with her nurses' aides, had developed a communication with Sylvia based on eye contact and smiles that allowed them to efficiently address any hint of discomfort on her face. Some of my sister's friends from her job also came to provide her with emotional support while she sat with my aunt Ginette in the row reserved for the family of the deceased. It was a calm atmosphere overall, and people strayed from the body in the casket to other areas in the room. The family was Catholic and very often someone would kneel in front of the coffin to offer a prayer—presumably on behalf of my mother.

Claude characteristically added some degree of sophistication to that emotionally trying night by bringing what I presumed to be some of my mother's favorite classical audio discs. Classical music provided a soothing background for the emotions that flooded that room, a guiding rhythm for the pulsations of our breasts. I wore a black tie given to me by a close friend the night before the wake. That was one of an infinite number of acts of kindness by an endless array of people that kept me sane throughout this ordeal.

Eventually, one woman who I presumed held a deacon position in the church began to sing a religious song in French to which the congregation responded to as a choir. She sang in a clear, sad, melancholic manner that reminded me of the Gregorian chants that used to awaken me as a child in my mother's house. The congregation answered her chants in unison with a harmonious melody of sadness and awe. It was sad and uplifting at the same time. I didn't fully understand the words, but I was moved. After several long minutes of this, the congregation spontaneously stopped singing, and a priest whom I had never met before walked up to a podium that was placed in the front of the room to give a eulogy.

He was a dark, handsome, middle-aged Haitian man who wore a traditional Roman Catholic priest's attire, consisting of a white collar under a black shirt and jacket. He spoke slowly, and the microphone carried his voice magnificently. He spoke in French, English, and Creole to satisfy everyone who gathered there. He spoke very well of my mother, which surprised me considering I couldn't remember ever meeting him. His face was not one that I could recall seeing in the hospital when my mother was sick. Nonetheless, he spoke of my mother almost as if he had regular contact with her. He spoke many good things about Sylvia, and I paid attention to each word spoken. I reasoned that if he hadn't known my mother personally he sure had done his research. I wondered whom he must have spoken to in order to say the things he said. As I listened to him, it dawned on me that he knew about my mother but didn't really know her.

After he spoke, he led us into a long prayer and told everyone when and where the funeral mass would be held. I saw people getting up to speak to one another once again and greet the immediate family before leaving. It bothered me that some in the audience didn't know who she was as a person and were getting it secondhand from someone who probably didn't know her either. I had a strong desire to have people see Sylvia through my eyes, to know her as I knew her. As the conversations began to get louder, I got up from my seat, walked toward the podium, and took the microphone. With my heart beating a little faster than usual, I asked everyone to please sit down because I had something I wanted to say. I think everyone except my sister who knew me best was surprised. After all, the service was over, and people were getting ready to go home. But they sat back in their seats and waited to hear what I had to say. The room became even quieter than when the priest was speaking. They gave me their full attention.

With my heart ready to burst out of my chest, I opened my mouth but found it difficult to speak. I hadn't cried since hearing of my mother's death, and as far as I was concerned, I think I was holding up pretty well. I was greeting everyone with a smile and being a good host in helping people to find seats. I hadn't even sat in the row reserved for the family of the deceased. I was wondering where my tears were and why I hadn't yet cried. The last thing I wanted to do was to burst out uncontrollably in front of everyone, but that was my fear. That would have been natural, I thought, but I didn't want to start crying then. I felt my eyes begin to moisten as I looked out into the audience. My knees began to feel weak, and a lump found its way into my throat. I opened my mouth again, and this time, thankfully, the words started coming out.

I invited the audience to see Sylvia through the eyes of her son. I spoke of her passion and undying love for her children, her sacrifices, and her shortcomings. I spoke of her temper and how she was never perfect but did the best she could with what she knew. I spoke of my mother as a pioneer, as someone who went ahead to the United States and forged a path for many to follow. Everyone but my sister had his or her eyes on me. Carline sat in the front with her eyes lowered. I think we both knew that if we had made eye contact I would have fallen apart. With each word I spoke, I knew that it was God Himself who gave me the strength to speak as I did.

I'm almost down the hill, and I still haven't found the gravesite. I begin to imagine that maybe someone moved it without notifying the family. That would be horrible. Who would move a whole gravesite without telling the family? No, that can't be it. Let me calm down and think about this. It has to be here. Let me see. That's the subway entrance right there, and the last time I was here I was standing at an angle that allowed me to see a street corner. I climb up and down little muddy hills, carefully watching the ground and reading the names on the plaques. I remember Claude saying that he had recently visited and placed some fresh flowers on the plaque, so I'm looking for a gravesite with flowers on it. The only problem is that almost every plaque has flowers on it. Thankfully, the drizzling has stopped. I go all the way down the hill to position myself in the same place I remembered the limousine had parked on the day of the funeral. If I can start from there and walk the same steps as I remember walking that day, I'm sure I'll be able to find the gravesite.

The limousine following the hearse on that cold winter day carried my mother's immediate family. This included my sister, uncle Maximilien and his daughter Catherine, aunts Ginette and Marijo, and me. Behind us spread a tail of friends and family members in other cars. The limousine had picked us up from Holy Cross Church in Brooklyn where the funeral was held.

From there, it had taken us to the borough of Queens, where we entered the Maple Grove Cemetery. After a few winding turns and an endless number of tombstones, plaques, and other memorials, we stopped where I believe I am presently standing. We waited in the limousine until several pallbearers from the funeral home carried the casket out of the hearse. A few moments later, we were all directed to the area where the casket would be buried and red roses were distributed to everyone by one of the pallbearers. We stood there on that cold February morning, with roses in our hands and many memories in our hearts.

Now if only I can follow the same path I took the last time I was at this cemetery. I begin walking in what I hope to be the correct path. There is something slightly familiar about this trail, something that seems to be tiptoeing quietly at the edge of my memory. With each step I take, the footsteps get louder. I walk a little faster now as the terrain begins to appear more and more familiar. Then I notice the grave plaque of my aunt Suzie who had died several years before. Yes! I'm in the right place! I go a little further, several plaques further. I see names of strangers, more dedications, and then…I see my grandmother's name. Next to hers, I see my mother's.

I stop walking and just stand there looking at the names. I look at them for several seconds before I fall to the muddy ground on my knees. To my surprise, the tears come, gushing like a river overrunning its bank. I'm not even sure why I'm crying, but I am so overwhelmed with emotions. I take my time, feeling the indentations on the plaque marking their names. I spell out their names slowly with my fingers, touching the plaque like a blind man reading braille. I read their names aloud to make the moment even more real, "Fernande Soliman…Sylvia Laroche Arty!" It means so much to have found this plaque.

In the course of a few moments, so much emotion pours out of me. I feel emptied, drained. I never truly realized how much I missed her. I had buried a major part of my soul with my mother on that cold February morning and seeing her name at this spot stirs every emotion in me. I arrange the roses in appropriate spots around the plaque while talking to two unseen spirits. I wipe the tears from my face and sit on the ground next to the plaque with my arms around my knees, feeling whole for the first time in more than a year. I don't know how long I sat there.

What is that warm sensation, gentle like a petal against my cheek? The sun is finally coming out. I look up, close my eyes, and breathe deeply, letting its warmth kiss my face. It's going to be a pleasant day.

Springtime in Brooklyn

I love the early spring. I once read a poem with the words "as the flowers in winter await the spring, my anguished soul slowly rises to sing."

That's how I feel this morning as I step out onto the street in Bay Ridge, Brooklyn— so alive that every cell in my body can taste the air and smell the season. I take a deep breath, enjoying the pleasure of the cool spring air making its way deep into my lungs. I could still hear the sounds of birds chirping on the branches of the trees that have only now begun to sprout budding green leaves. The morning sky is so beautifully clear and blue that I stare at it for a moment, admiring this perfect painting that can only reflect the glory of a Creator. *What a Saturday morning*, I think. *Makes a person grateful to be alive.*

I woke up this morning at dawn and decided to take an early morning walk. This usually happens to me in the beginning of spring when I can't seem to continue sleeping after the sun rises. I don't know if it has to do with my body adjusting to the change in the season or the fact that the birds wake me up with their chirping. But I woke up and decided to take a walk just to enjoy the freshness of a new day.

I'm wearing a blue sweater and a green baseball cap as I start my walk on Sixty-fifth Street, heading toward Fourth Avenue. I pass under the Gowanus Expressway—my nightmare every weekday morning. It always seems to be under construction whenever I need to get somewhere quickly. I try to avoid the pigeon poop covering the street under the expressway and make my way to Sixtieth Street. There aren't many cars on the road at this time of the morning, and I'm enjoying the stillness and silence of these early hours. There are only a few people standing at the bus stop on Sixtieth Street, and I greet them with a smile and a "Good morning!" as I pass.

The brownstones lining Sixtieth Street are all designed the same way, with nice rows of steps where the residents can sit and socialize with their neighbors if they choose. An old man is outside in his bathrobe, smoking a cigarette on his stoop. Soon children will be playing games on these streets while their parents sit on the stoops watching them.

When I reach Fourth Avenue, I decide to walk a bit further, still savoring the calm and solitude of the morning. I cross the street and notice a young man, walking ahead of me with a familiar stride. From behind, he appears slightly overweight and disheveled with the tail of his yellow shirt sticking out of his baggy blue jeans. His sneakers look dirty, and I notice that they are not laced appropriately. His hair is in the style of a short Afro.

I pick up my pace and walk a little faster. When I catch up to him, I take a look at him from the side to confirm my suspicions. "Hello, Jojo," I say. "Boy, I haven't seen you in a while. What's up?"

I startle him, but he recovers quickly and looks at me with a wide grin. I see on his unshaven face the smile of the boy I knew so long ago.

"Hi, Pierre Richard. What are you doing up so early? I thought doctors sleep pretty late on Saturdays," he says with a smile. "Do you have to work at a clinic?"

"No," I respond. "I just wanted to take a walk. Where are you heading to this early in the morning?" I know Jojo lives a block away from me with his parents, and I'm wondering if he was sent on an errand.

"I'm going to the mental health clinic near Maimonides Hospital. The doctor changed my medication, and it seems to be doing me good. It's making me gain weight, but I don't feel stiff like the last few medications I was on."

We walk together sharing some small talk, and I remember the last time I met Jojo. I was a second-year resident in psychiatry at the Kings County Hospital, and it was a busy night at the "G" building. I can still hear the sounds of that night.

———— ◆•◆•◆ ————

Klick-ka pick! The sound of the big skeleton key was loud as it turned clockwise to lock the door on the G-53 psychiatric unit. I pushed at the door to make sure that it was locked. You can never underestimate the need for security and safety while working in a psychiatric hospital.

Like the patients I treat, nights on call at Kings County Psychiatric Hospital were often unpredictable. Some nights you wondered if there was a full moon outside, and this night was one of them. Leaving the unit, I could still hear threats coming from the tall, large-framed, middle-aged man whom I had been forced to medicate after he, without any apparent provocation, struck a fellow patient in the face. No matter what we said to him, he wouldn't calm down. Even as the nurses' aides were trying to prevent him from striking out at anyone else, he continued to yell, "You just wait till I get out of here! I'll kill you, Doctor! I'll kill you!" I hoped that he would forget me by the time I returned to that particular unit.

As a psychiatric resident, I provided care for all of the psychiatric in-patients in addition to the patients in our emergency room. While taking care of the violent patient on the unit, I received a page from the nurse in the emergency room, letting me know that there were now five additional patients waiting to be evaluated, including one who apparently asked for me by name. Between me and the other two residents on call that day, we had already admitted eight patients, and it didn't look as if the flow of patients would ever stop.

The psychiatric hospital was an old building, looking more like a medieval castle than a New York hospital. A large skeleton key was needed to get to almost every treatment area of the hospital. Sometimes, I would laugh thinking that the only difference between the patients and the doctors was possession of this key. The elevators needed live operators to work them, and as it is with old elevators in very old buildings, they were used by a large volume of people throughout the day, resulting in a frequent need for servicing. I waited for one impatiently on the fifth-floor area outside the psychiatric unit, debating whether I should just take the stairs. I decided to save my energy and wait.

It was quiet in that corridor—quiet enough to fool an uninitiated observer into thinking the units were also quiet. I waited for what seemed like an eternity. The humming of the elevator cords told me that it was working, but the door never quite got around to opening. I decided to end the suspense and took the stairs. Arriving at the lobby, I headed straight for the emergency room.

The emergency room was busy with nurses performing triage on the new arrivals, medical students doing physical exams and evaluating patients, and doctors going over medication orders. There were also several patients sitting with their family members in a small waiting area, each hoping to be the next person seen.

"Hey, Doc. Where have you been? The attending is looking for you," a nurse said to me.

I looked around for the attending doctor, who was also my supervisor that night, and found him sitting at a table reviewing the admission charts. "I'm glad you're the one on call tonight, Doc, 'cause we've got a patient in the single room who came in here pretty excited and asking for you. He says he knows you personally. We have him sitting in the waiting area. Go take a look at him and let me know what he has to say."

Leaving the attending doctor, I went to find the patient.

As I entered the waiting room, I was startled to hear someone calling out my name in Creole, "Pierre Richard…Pierre Richard!"

The only people who call me by my full name are family members and close friends from Haiti. With everyone else, it's "Pierre." So it came as a surprise that someone in the emergency room would address me like this. Not recognizing the voice, I turned to see who was calling me, and I almost didn't recognize the young man sitting with the other patients in the waiting room. I approached this young man with a round friendly face and a smile, and it was only when my eyes met his that my mind made some degree of recognition.

Before I could say hello and ask any questions, he asked, "Hey, Pierre Richard, how are you? It's good to see you. My mom told me that you work here, and I was hoping to see you." That's when I recognized Jojo, someone I hadn't seen since the fifth or sixth grade.

Jojo. That incredible bright light I had known as an adolescent and assumed was going to become a rocket scientist or something similar. Surprisingly, I had been either unable or unwilling to make the connection that would have explained his presence in the psychiatric emergency room. My memory was stuck on the quiet boy with intelligent eyes who always had interesting comments to make on every issue discussed between children in their preadolescent years.

I remembered the boy who used to go on family trips with me. I thought about how close our mothers had always been. Although I had lost contact with Jojo, I always assumed he was doing well in school. Meeting him in the patient waiting area of the psychiatric emergency room was the last place that I would think of seeing JoJo again.

I asked him a question that seemed obvious yet needed to be asked, "Jojo, what are you doing here?"

"Well, Pierre Richard, I was really going crazy at home," he responded with a rueful smile. "I was screaming for no reason, feeling really anxious and afraid. My mom got scared and called the ambulance. I was really out of control. She didn't come on the ambulance with me this time. She stayed home with my father."

"What happened to get you so upset?" I asked him.

"I don't know, Pierre Richard. Every once in a while, something happens that I can't help. I get anxious. They say I have schizophrenia. It started when I was in college. Doctors try to help me by giving me these medications, but they all have some kind of side effect. Sometimes they find something that really works well for me, but then it stops working, and I'm left with just the side effects. And some of them make me gain weight."

Jojo proceeded to tell me more about the problems with the medications he was taking.

As he was speaking to me, I found myself reflecting on how unpredictable life was. To have met again after such a long time, at this point in our lives, was a difficult experience to describe. Years ago, he was a childhood friend, but that night he was a psychiatric patient speaking to a psychiatric resident.

I vaguely remembered sitting at home during a visit from college and hearing my mother tell me he wasn't well. As a matter of fact, he had to drop out because he couldn't seem to find the volition to continue with the demands of a four-year college education. At the time I had been hearing but not listening. Somehow I had stored it in my memory and found myself listening that night to what was heard years ago.

I was so enthralled seeing Jojo that I had forgotten about everything else, including the need to begin filling out the many forms required for each patient.

I said, "Jojo…I have to leave you for a moment to go get some forms. I'll come back to speak to you in a moment."

"No problem, Pierre Richard. I know you're busy. I think I'll be here for a while." After all these years, he still had a good sense of humor considering what he has been going through.

Jojo asks me about several friends that we knew as children while walking with him. I tell him how the ones I have kept in contact with are, even as I am pleasantly surprised at the accuracy of his memory. He goes on to remind me of the times that different jokes were made during our family outings and who said them. We share some laughter together, remembering those young days filled with the innocent excitement of childhood. While walking, I begin to notice a few dark clouds gathering together overhead, as if getting ready to rain. *That's strange…I didn't hear anything having to do with rain today*, I think. I ignore the clouds and continue with our conversation. It is a pleasant walk, and the company is good. I walk a little longer than I had planned, getting close to Eighth Avenue.

As we walk, I ask about his plans for school, and he says, "I don't really want to finish school. When I was in college, it was getting harder and harder to concentrate. Now it's like I don't want to be bothered."

"Did you ever have any problems with hearing voices in your head?" I ask him. I can't remember ever having asked him that question before, but somehow while walking along this morning, the question seems to flow right in with the conversation.

"No," he responded. Then after a moment, he said, "I know that some people have that experience, but that hasn't happened to me."

I go on to ask Jojo about his family, and he tells me about his father. Being a stern man with firm, traditional ways of seeing the world, his father has difficulties dealing with Jojo's illness. This difficulty manifests in his impatience with his son and the things he says to him.

Jojo says to me, "Sometimes my father yells at me when I stay in bed most of the day. He wants me to go to school or get a job, but I can't do that right now. He says that I'm lazy, but I can't do it. I can't concentrate on that right now. I love him 'cause he's my father, but sometimes I get really tired of him."

I reason to myself that Jojo's family, like most Haitian families, place a strong value on education. The general belief is that education is the key to advancement in life, and Jojo's father may have simply felt that Jojo wasn't taking advantage of the opportunities available in the United States.

The clouds have come together now, and I can't see the sun. I'm surprised to feel the gentle moisture of raindrops on my head and face. I look at Jojo, and he doesn't seem bothered by the gentle drops.

I look up and recognize the fruit stand on Fort Hamilton Parkway and decide I should turn back and head for home. Jojo looks at me and says that his clinic is only a few blocks away.

"Jojo, it's been really good talking to you. I hope that whatever medication the doctor decides to give you helps. I'm gonna head back home now."

"Yeah, I enjoyed talking to you this morning. Can I have your number to call you every once in a while? Sometimes I just want to have someone I can talk to."

"Sure, but I don't have any place I can write it down right now," I say while searching my pocket for a pen or pencil.

Jojo takes a pen from his pocket and writes my number on his hand. "Thanks, Pierre Richard, I'll call you sometime."

We shake hands, and I watch Jojo walk away from me with his loosely laced sneakers and yellow shirt sticking out from his baggy blue jeans. The rain is coming down harder now, bouncing off Jojo's head, and causing him to walk a little faster. Like me, he has also left home this morning without an umbrella. I turn my head and begin my walk back home, thinking of Jojo and how unpredictable life can be.

The Fiery Furnace

I looked at my watch and realized with a sense of hopeless resignation that it was 2:30 a.m. Getting to sleep was becoming a lost cause. Approximately ten minutes earlier, a nurse on nursing station A-11 had paged me to report that an IV had just come out of another patient's arm. After examining and eventually admitting three prior patients with various medical problems, I had dared to entertain the possibility that I would be able to get some rest, but rest was becoming more of an elusive abstract than a concrete reality. After inserting what seemed like the hundredth IV, I began to suspect that the nurses were conspiring against me.

It was November 1990. I was working the night shift, on call at Kings County Hospital in Brooklyn, and trying to live through my first year of hell—otherwise known as a "medical residency."

From the first night on call, I slowly came to realize what my life would be like for the next three years. During the transition from medical student to intern, time suddenly took on a new meaning and became loose change in a pocket full of holes. I never knew where I lost it. I was convinced that a day was far less than the twenty-four hours I was used to before starting the residency program.

There was never a shortage of patients to treat. Day and night, they entered the emergency room with all types of ailments. Although they came from many different countries, the faces all spoke the same language of pain, and their eyes all expressed hope as they looked at the doctors and nurses in white coats. At times, this responsibility was overwhelming. I tried not to dwell on the feelings of apprehension and loneliness that accompanied me to the hospital every night like faithful friends.

I quickly glanced over at the patient as I walked into the small single-bed on A-11. With a heavy sigh, I realized this intravenous was going to take a while. The patient was an elderly black woman, possibly in her late seventies, who looked very emaciated. She rested quietly on her back, her eyes closed, and I presumed she was asleep. Her thin frail arms were above the bed sheet that covered her body, and from a distance, I couldn't detect any veins that would readily surrender to a needle and catheter. The wool hat that covered what I suspected to be a balding head gave me an indication that she was

61

most probably a cancer patient receiving chemotherapy. I was to find out later from her chart that her admission was a last desperate attempt to arrest a rapidly spreading ovarian cancer.

After examining this latest obstacle to my rest, I went to look for the catheter and tubing needed to insert the IV. Coming back into the small, dimly lit room, I experienced a sudden sense of peace and comfort as I turned on the lights. Most of the patients' rooms that I had visited had either a framed representation of a famous painting on one of the walls installed by the administration and meant to help alleviate the anxiety about being in the hospital, or one or two personal pictures of someone special to the patient sitting on a dresser. This room was different. The walls were decorated with various get-well cards signed by family members and friends. On a chair next to the patient's bed were two carefully folded blankets. Above the old sink, pictures of several smiling children were taped to the wall, and a thick Bible sat on the dresser, close to her bed. It was worn and obviously well used, with torn pieces at the edges of its black cover and inner pages.

I looked over at the patient again. She had awakened, and our eyes met. I introduced myself, "Good morning, Ma'am, I'm the doctor on call. I'm sorry to wake you, but I came to replace your IV."

She winced in pain while removing the sheet from across her body and responded with a surprisingly strong voice, "You didn't wake me, young man. The nurses told me to expect you. I just couldn't sleep thinking about that needle going back into my arm. My Lord, as often as they put those things in my arm, I just can't get used to it. Well, let's get this over with. Why don't you put those blankets on my bed so you can sit down and be comfortable?" She pointed at her chair. "It's so hard to find my veins you know."

Looking at her thin arms, I knew she was telling the truth. There were multiple puncture marks on both her hands and arms, evidence of previous unsuccessful attempts. As I was examining her arms, looking carefully for an access, she again let out a silent moan of pain, and my eyes fell to her face. It was a haggard, tired-looking, wrinkle-scarred face. The sum of all her life's troubles and afflictions were etched in each wrinkle. But her eyes and smile told an entirely different story. Looking at them, I didn't see any evidence of turmoil. What I saw was a vibrant woman inside, touching the world outside with a smile.

"I hope you're good and don't have to poke around too much to find my veins," she said, breaking my stare.

"Ma'am," I replied, "I don't intend to hurt you any more than I have to, but if I find a vein quickly, it'll be a miracle."

"Well, son, just do what you have to do."

After a few moments of palpating her arms and doing all I could to bring a vein to the surface, I said, "Are you ready, Ma'am? I think I may have found a vein here."

"Go on. I've been through worse than this," she replied. Her courage was admirable, but unfortunately for the both of us, her veins were not. Her small vein couldn't tolerate the intrusion of the catheter and decided to collapse instead. This meant that I wasn't going to get to sleep for a little while longer, of course.

"Ma'am, I'm afraid I'm going to have to hurt you again. Your vein didn't take the catheter."

"Son," she began saying, "through all this chemotherapy, the vomiting, the radiation, seeing my hair fall out…my Lord and Savior Jesus the Christ has kept me going. I know as sure as I'm speaking to you now that He'll bring me through this little fire. I don't like getting stuck, but I need my medication. So you best just try again or come back later when you catch yourself some rest."

I was blown away by what she said and how she said it. This sick person was telling me, the young healthy doctor, to come back later after I "catch some rest." Did someone suddenly reverse our roles without telling me? Even as these thoughts went through my mind, the strength and resolve coming from this wasted-looking woman commanded my attention. I wondered about the source of her vitality in the face of a slow and miserable death.

Up to that year of my life, I had witnessed people dying in various ways: quietly, loudly, with much anger, and peacefully, but never with a smile. To face death head-on, day after agonizing day, and to still have the fortitude this woman had was beyond my understanding. She was an enigma. The multiple puncture marks on her thin arms spoke of a daily agony caused by physical intrusions. Her wool hat told me tales of side effects and disappointing treatment failures. And her painfully limited mobility reflected the burden of chronic aches and pains on a body rejecting its host. But her voice resonated with an inner fortitude and faith that was far beyond my understanding. She startled me from my drowsiness and commanded my attention. I felt a compelling desire to get to know her, befriend her, and learn from her. She did not disappoint me.

In the nights that followed, I took several opportunities to visit her, not only to see how she was doing, but also (and this surprised me) to capture some of her encouragement and strength. It was only too easy for me to be discouraged by the thought that someone might die as a result of a mistake I may make due to lack of sleep, poor diet, or constant stress. With these thoughts in mind, I appreciated her encouragement even more.

I would enter her dark and peaceful room like the very first night, and without saying a word, she would usher me in. "How's it going tonight, Doc? They keeping you busy enough? Now don't you worry any. God Himself has put you here for a reason, and he sure ain't gonna leave you now. Remember how he delivered those three Jewish boys from that fiery furnace? That King Nebuchadnezzar looked in that furnace and saw four men in there, not three. And then he said the fourth man looked like the Son of God. Son, that means that God is in there with us, in the middle of our troubles. He's no respecter of persons. What he did for those three Jewish boys, he'll do for us if we're servin' him. There ain't any trouble or furnace hot enough that he can't deliver you from. You just keep that in mind."

Well, there I was, a medical intern, a physician supposedly endowed with the knowledge to alleviate sickness, being comforted and encouraged by an old woman dying of cancer. Can you spell *humility*, Doctor? It starts with an *H*. This woman helped me put my intern year in focus when I couldn't even see beyond my next admission. She never gave me the impression that she was too weak to give me a portion of what was left of her strength. I began to look forward to the nights on call when I would take a break from either admitting patients or writing orders, and go to her room. There I would sit and listen to countless stories of how good her God had been to her. Once in a while, for maybe a second or two, I somehow imagined that I could see beyond that frail old body and actually get a glimpse of her essence, her light, the radiance that was truly her.

On one exceptionally busy night, something very interesting happened in that peaceful little room. I decided to rest momentarily in what had now become my favorite chair in the hospital. I quietly entered her room. Since she didn't greet me as she was accustomed to doing and her light was turned off, I assumed she was asleep and decided to just sit and close my eyes for a few seconds. When I opened my eyes, I was surprised to see this sickly woman sitting up in her bed in the darkness.

To my recollection, I had never seen her sit up, and I had reasoned that due to the spread of the cancer to her bones, every physical movement must lead to excruciating pain. And then it dawned on me that I was unknowingly involved in her incentive to sit up. While sitting up in bed, her thin arms and opened hands were stretched out in my direction. She looked like she was either about to give me something or present me to someone. Her eyes remained tightly shut while her lips were quietly moving, as if holding a conversation with someone in silent whispers. After a moment, she raised both hands toward the ceiling, looked up, and opened her eyes with a look of triumph or jubilation. She had been praying.

She was praying for me with all the passion and fervor her small frame could rouse. Actually, she might have been praying for world peace and everyone from Brooklyn to Miami, but I knew I was on that prayer list. When she finished praying, she quietly lay back in bed and covered her torso with her blanket. She was apparently exhausted and in pain, but her face, even in the poor lighting, appeared very content. I didn't pay much attention to the words of her prayer, and I couldn't hear them even if I had wanted to. I didn't respond to her in any way. My unresponsiveness was not due to fear or rudeness. I was just so captivated by the moment. All I could do was sit back and wonder. The sound of my beeper reminded me that I was still on call.

Several nights later, I was busier than usual, replacing intravenous and nasogastric tubes and responding to various complaints of chest and abdominal pain. After the morning rounds with my attending physician, the only thing on my mind was to get home and go to sleep.

One morning, I decided to stop by and see how my favorite patient was doing. After all, I had interrupted her rest enough times at night, so I thought I might as well visit her in the morning before I went home. On the way to her room, I couldn't help but smile thinking about how surprised she was going to be to see me in the daytime. Halfway down the hall on A-11, I could see the entrance to her room. I entered her room and opened my mouth to say, "Good mornin', young lady," but the words never came. The room was empty.

Inside my head, in the deepest cavern of my mind, a little voice was whispering a secret I didn't want to hear. As quickly as it spoke, I muffled it. Maybe the nurses had moved her to another room. Maybe she was discharged to spend her last days with her family. So many *maybes* were racing through my mind, but my heart already knew the truth.

With my chest beating, I walked over to the nurses' station. "Good morning. Where is the patient in room ten?" I asked.

"Oh, she died three days ago. Her family came in yesterday to pick up her belongings. Were you her doctor?"

"No," I replied. "She was my friend."

A well of emotion stirred within me. "Why did she have to die now?" I asked myself. I felt a very deep sadness. Leaving the hospital, I passed through the pediatric emergency room. I was deaf to the sound of screaming children. I saw their crying faces but could not hear their cries. I was a walking bag of anger. I was angry with myself for not being there when she died. Why didn't I go to see her earlier? She died three days ago. Was I really that busy?

By the time I got home, I couldn't think and didn't want to deal with any emotions. I finally found rest in the gentle and comforting arms of sleep. As my consciousness slowly succumbed to sleep's consoling embrace, my last thoughts were that I would not see my friend again for a very long time.

Through the years, I have come to realize the reason for my anger. I was angry with this woman for dying after I came to care for her. I have also come to appreciate the treasure that she gave me—the lesson she laced into my life. For so many of us, death is a fearful, painful territory. To traverse this territory—even to approach it by any means—can be a psychologically and emotionally traumatic experience. This we understand almost instinctively. The idea that one day we will leave this life is very unsettling. But to face one's death through a slow, physically deteriorating and painful disease and yet daily express love goes beyond our base instincts. This elderly woman stepped out of her pain and showed a young intern the power of hope in something far greater than death, deeper than despair, and stronger than ourselves. It is a hope that is sure to quench the scorching flames of any fiery furnace.

Grace

When I set out for work this morning, it never occurred to me that my day would involve a middle-aged woman standing over me with a cane, apparently ready to hit me. But here I am in my office at the Kings County Hospital Chemical Dependency Services, being threatened by a heroin addict whom I have been treating for the past two years.

Today Magdalena appears much older than her stated age of fifty. Droplets of sweat cover her forehead, and each wrinkle on her face tells a story of a different tragedy, a different man, but the same old drug. Her eyes, usually painted with the colors of sadness and weariness, are now replaced with a deep hue of intense anger. Under her eyelids are deep grooves chiseled by years of poor sleep combined with tears. She hardly has any teeth left but has never made the time to see a dentist. With each word that she blurts at me, I smell that familiar scent of alcohol. Did I forget to mention that she was also alcohol dependent? The grey suit she is wearing is filthy and emits the scent of alcohol. She carries a medical diagnosis of hepatitis with the unfortunate consequence of liver cirrhosis. In addition, she has a mental diagnosis of clinical depression.

Magdalena has just burst into my office, angry that I didn't speak to her an hour ago when her visiting nurse's aide called me to say that Magdalena smelled strongly of alcohol and was talking about killing herself. I had advised the aide to call 911 and have Magdalena taken to the nearest psychiatric emergency room for an evaluation. After passing on that advice, the aide informed me that Magdalena had jumped out of her bed and ran out of the shelter apartment. I had a strong impression that she might come to my office, but I wasn't sure.

"Do you know what I've been through? Do you? Do you have any idea what I'm going through? How dare you tell my aide to take me to a psychiatric hospital! You're a doctor! You should have gotten your ass off that chair and spoken to me! You didn't even speak to me! What do you think? You think I'm crazy? Do you?" Magdalena hurls these words at me even as I try to sit calmly in my chair. I know that in her angry drunken state, if I stand up immediately, she may interpret my standing up as a hostile act, and there is no telling what her reaction might be. I am also trying to keep my own anger in check.

"Magdalena, please sit down," I say firmly as I rise slowly to meet her. "I see that you're upset, but this is not going to help us come to any understanding. I do want to talk to you, but I can't do it with you yelling at me. Besides, that cane you're holding onto makes me feel like you're going to hit me."

By this time the security officers who had heard her loud yelling have finally arrived outside my door and want to know what is going on. Magdalena decides to sit in the chair I had offered her a few seconds ago.

"Doc, you okay?" one of the officers asks from the corridor.

I open the door and respond, "Yes, everything is fine." They look understandably doubtful. "All right, Doc, if you say so. But if you need us, we're right outside. Just give a holler."

"Thanks. I'll call you if I need you," I say, closing the door.

The moment the door closes, Magdalena's face undergoes a metamorphosis. Her face changes from intense anger to sadness in the span of a few seconds. She slowly begins to cry. As I sit in the chair opposite her, I notice that she doesn't just smell of alcohol, she reeks of it. It is as if every pore is oozing the stuff. The room begins to smell of it. At this point, I'm not sure who is crying, her or the alcohol.

Eventually, she takes out a picture of a woman and shows it to me as if I should have known who it was. I take the picture from her coarse trembling fingers for a closer examination. The woman in the picture appears to be in her early twenties, very attractive with a military uniform on. The background shows an American flag, so common in those military-type pictures. I detect a bit of resemblance to Magdalena in the smile.

With tears making their way down her cheeks, she tells me what I had already begun to suspect. "Doc, I'm so worried about my daughter. She's in Iraq, and she called the other night to talk to me. I ain't heard from her since. I'm so worried about her…worried sick… not knowing if she's dead or alive. It's the not knowing that eats at my heart, makes it hurt at night. The last thing she said to me was that they were going on a mission. That was two days ago."

She stops talking for a moment and lowers her head. I take the opportunity to ask her for her cane. She smiles, wipes her face with the palm of her right hand, and says, "Don't worry, Doc. I wasn't goin' to hit you with this. I'm not as crazy as you think. I ain't lookin' to get into any loony bin."

Disregarding her assurance, I take the cane from her and place it behind my chair. I explain to her that I have a responsibility to her to do whatever is needed to assure her safety. And if that means recommending psychiatric hospitalization, then I will do just that.

She responds with, "Yeah, whatever," while brushing off my argument with a wave of her right hand.

I invite her to talk about her daughter. She responds by looking at my face as if for the very first time. She pauses and leans her head back against the wall, looks up at the ceiling, and exhales. When she speaks, her words begin to guide me through a world of hurt and addiction that has been her life for nearly thirty years. Like a voyeur, I watch the painful events surrounding the birth of her daughter, using her words as my eyes.

⚬•◦◈◦•⚬

She could hear her own labored breathing and feel her lungs expand with each breath. She had been watching her belly grow with much wonder and enthusiasm in the past eight months but had never seen herself so huge. This wasn't how she had planned to spend her afternoon. The contractions were coming faster now, and she knew the baby wanted to come out. There were two nurses, each holding a hand on either side of the bed, and a midwife had just finished cleaning the area under her buttocks. She had inadvertently defecated while trying to push against the contractions. A clean sheet was placed under her, and her eyes closed against both the embarrassment of defecating and the physical strain of the contractions. "I'm sorry… I'm sorry," she said between breaths. "I couldn't help it."

"Don't you worry, honey. You just keep on pushing," responded the midwife. "I can almost see the head now. Just give a little more push."

The contractions were coming stronger and faster, and with each effort, she felt that her head was about to explode.

Earlier that day, Magdalena had picked up the last two bags of heroin from her dealer and couldn't wait to get back to her apartment in downtown Brooklyn, and go shoot it in the bathroom. The memory of that morning kept on playing in the recorder of her mind as Magdalena lay on the hospital bed, bathed in perspiration, panting as if she had just run a marathon.

She felt the euphoria course through her veins, spill into her brain like the soft sensations after a long night with the gentlest lover. Her eyes rolled back as her neck muscles loosened up and her head went back. Nothing mattered for the next few hours except this feeling, this state, this...ecstasy. She didn't even feel the cold hard tiles that lined the bathroom floor against her skin, nor the cool breeze of the January air that swept between the cracks of the old window sitting above the dirty toilet bowl. She was everywhere and nowhere at once, riding a cloud of good feelings brought on by the syringe still sticking out of her left forearm. "Please, Lord, just protect my baby. Please, Lord, don't let nothin' happen to my baby," she cried with her last remnants of coherence.

This was how Magdalena started her morning all those years ago, by getting her daily fix of heroin. Without it, she was sure the pain of withdrawal would make her lose her baby, kill her, or both. She was eight months pregnant and wanted desperately to bring this baby into existence.

Even as she began to lose consciousness, her memories took her to the first time she felt the baby move inside her and knew that she wanted to have it...protect it. It was the only positive thing she could cling to in the miserable life she lived on this godforsaken planet.

She was told a million times how her drug abuse might injure the baby in her womb, but she just couldn't help it. The heroin had called her by name. It knew where she lived, where she slept, where she prayed, even what she thought. She had been addicted since her boyfriend introduced her to it at the age of twenty-two. That was ten years ago, and she was never able to stop using it. During the course of the years, she tried her share of alcohol, marijuana, and some crack;

but nothing rocked her world like dope. It was to her the sweetest ecstasy, her faithful friend in times of need. It was there when she was angry, anxious, lonely, and especially during her depressive moods. Nothing took away her hurts and made her forget like heroin.

Of course, there were the occasional periods of abstention, but she continued to use. She became involved in several rehabilitation programs, but that was only to satisfy intrusive family members and bosses who, as far as she was concerned, were making a big deal out of nothing. Besides, the most these programs did was reduce the intensity of the calling by filling her mind with other voices. But the calling was always there, like the hunger of starving children who forget the gnawing of their stomachs but know they need to feed.

After she had lost several well-paying jobs and found herself living in a shelter with a verbally abusive boyfriend, she began to think seriously about the possibility that her life was out of control. Several months went by, and she discovered that she was pregnant.

Magdalena then quickly enrolled in a methadone to abstinence program. This provided her with a measured amount of methadone in order to reduce the physical urge for the heroin. She had formed an idea that if she were able to have this baby, her life would come to mean something. She had tried to explain this to her boyfriend; but he just laughed at her, and eventually left, unable to convince her to get an abortion.

His leaving made her more depressed, but for the first months, she was good. She participated in the groups, which she attended daily and was even willing to see a psychiatrist for her depression. She made it clear to the doctor from the very beginning that she was not crazy; she just needed someone to speak with from time to time. The sessions were helpful, and on several occasions, she was surprised to find herself crying.

However, this honeymoon lasted for only five to six months. The heroin kept calling her name and even invaded her dreams. For several weeks, she would awaken in the middle of the night shaking and sweating as if she had a fever. Eventually, she was unable to sleep at all. She knew what would help her enter the most comfortable sleep but refused to listen to any such thoughts as she, for the first time in a very long time, had a priority in her heart greater than her urge. She discussed this with her counselor, who recommended an increase in her dosage of methadone. This helped a little. But the urge to use accompanied her home every day, had dinner, and slept with her every night. It lived in her neighborhood, stood on each familiar block, and waited for her to pass by to offer her a cheap and quick piece of heaven. She was able to find other routes to get home and avoid as many dealers as possible, but as the months passed, the urge began to draw her back.

It wanted her and made itself part of the very air that she breathed. There were nights that she cried out in the darkness, to whatever God might be listening. She cried for help, for the sake of the baby. Her silent tears pouring out were the only response she received. Soon her attendance at the program became less consistent, and occasionally, heroin was found in her urine. Her psychiatrist noticed her change in mood, but she became less able to keep consistent appointments. Unable to leave the heroin even for the sake of the growing child in her womb, she was resigned to surrender.

Earlier today, on the way home from his office, she was hit by a car and sent flying into the air. Bystanders would later go home to talk about the obviously pregnant woman who had gotten up after being hit by a car and refused any medical attention. They would call her crazy, but none knew of the voice that promised her soothing bliss for her aches if she would just get up off the concrete and head toward her apartment.

When she arrived home, she fell into a heroin stupor after inserting the syringe into her vein. The contractions awakened her with a sensation of wetness between her legs. She was able to crawl from the bathroom floor into the adjoining room, reach for the phone, and dial 911. After breaking down her door, the ambulance drivers took her to the nearest hospital emergency room as fast as they could. She was taken into the Labor and Delivery area immediately.

After a quick examination, the doctors decided there was no time for an enema or any form of anesthesia. The baby needed to come out. Her clothes and underwear were quickly removed and replaced with a white hospital gown. Even in the midst of this experience, she still had the taste of heroin on her mind.

The nurse wiped her sweaty forehead with a towel as Magdalena continued to strain under the force of the contractions. Magdalena heard the nurse to the left of her say, "It's okay, honey, you're doing fine. We're going to be right here with you to help you bring your little one home. Just don't give up."

But giving up was exactly what she had already done. She had given up on herself years ago, and then she gave up on the baby. She felt as if her back was about to break in half with the strain of the contractions, and her facial contortions reflected the pain. She didn't believe she was going to be able to bring her baby forth. She opened her eyes wide, and with tears running down her sunken cheeks, she screamed, "Oh God, help me! I can't do this!"

This time, there was an answer in the dark. The midwife standing between her open legs looked at her and calmly asked, "Magdalena, if you can't do this, then who is going to do it for you? The baby's head is looking at me. If you can't do this, then we will need to take you in for an emergency C-section."

Magdalena had noticed that the doctor in the room had his eyes fixed on the fetal monitor. She felt as if she was about to faint and found it ridiculous that at her weakest moment she was being asked to try her hardest. With that thought, laughter arose from deep inside her and found its way along her vocal cords and out of her mouth. She began to laugh, which surprisingly made her feel stronger, and as the two nurses on both sides of her body held her up to help her brace herself, she gave another push and kept on pushing. With eyes wide open and her face in a grimace of determination, she pushed. She pushed against the pain between her legs, against the last effects of the heroin, against all the darkness of her life.

For several seconds, she felt as if someone had turned off the oxygen, and her head was about to burst. It was then that she remembered going deaf and the room becoming dark. She fell back against a pillow and waited.

For what felt like an eternity, she waited. She waited for what all new mothers wait for, the sound of her baby crying. As her hearing came back and the light returned to her eyes, she heard the long-awaited cry. With tears in her eyes, she raised her head to see her child, and the baby was brought to her, wrapped in a white towel. The newborn was placed next to her bosom since she was too tired to hold the infant.

"You have a healthy baby girl, Magdalena, congratulations!" the midwife said.

"What is the child's name?" asked the doctor. Magdalena looked at the baby and, without hesitation, said, "Grace, her name is Grace."

———◦✦◦———

I feel captivated by Magdalena's story. She has never spoken as clearly and coherently as I am hearing her this morning. For a moment, I feel as if I were in that delivery room with her. I don't interrupt her. "That's right, Doc. Her name is Grace. She's my miracle baby," she says, pointing at the picture in my hand. "With all the drugs I was doin', it's a miracle she was born at all. But she was born. And born healthy too! A little early but, by the grace of God, healthy. I hear preachers and priests talk about the grace of God, but I know it firsthand. I really had no right to have her and to have her healthy at that. I didn't even have the right to hope for a healthy baby. But she was given to me perfect. I don't think you can understand what I'm tryin' to say to you, Doc. You see, even in the darkest hole that I ever found myself in…God met me there. He listened to me and answered my prayer. He protected my baby in spite of me and, for that, I'm grateful. I know I made some bad choices in my life, but none of them was God's fault. And now I'm waiting for God to bring my baby back home."

Once again, I look at the picture in my hand. After some silence, I return the picture to those coarse trembling hands, and Magdalena motions for her cane.

"Well, Doc, that's all you'll get out of me today. That's my story, and I'm sticking to it. I didn't really want to kill myself. I just want my baby home. When can I come to talk to you again?"

We talk a little more about the war and how she is waiting to hear her daughter's voice. I comment on how painful that must be, and she responds by saying, "Doc, you don't know the half of it. I haven't been eatin' or sleepin'. Just worryin' about my daughter."

I know I can't allow her to go home in the drunk and depressed state she's in. I discuss with her the possibility of being hospitalized in order to give her body and mind time to heal from her recent binge.

"As long as I get to talk to you every once in a while," she says.

I return her cane to her from behind my chair and say, "Of course you will Magdalena. I wouldn't want you coming back next time so angry that you actually hit me." She laughs at my response, and we begin walking toward the registration area for the inpatient detox. She begins to speak more freely with less tension in her voice.

"Doc, trust me on this one. I ain't ready yet to go to the flip side. I know that I have my issues, but I been through too much to give up now. Just don't give up on me, 'cause God sure hasn't given up on me yet." She gives me a wink.

"No, Magdalena, I won't give up on you. If God has kept you all this time, the least I can do is to believe in you," I respond.

She laughs and moves a little closer to me.

House Calls

"Code red! 9 West! Code red!" I ran up the remaining five flights of stairs to the ninth floor of the Brooklyn Veterans Administration Hospital as the litany sounded through the stairwell. With my heart beating so hard, I could hear the pounding in my ears. I rushed into the small private room on 9 West where the code team had already assembled.

"Whose patient is this?" I demanded. "Does someone have his chart?"

"Here's the chart, Doc," said a nurse, handing me a chart. "The patient's intern is gone for the day. He's not on the do-not-resuscitate list," the nurse added, gesturing at the patient. "He was found lying in bed without a pulse and not breathing about three minutes ago."

"Who's the code leader?" the supervising nurse asked.

"I am," I said. "I'm the medical senior today. Continue with the compressions until the EKG monitor is hooked up to the patient. Does the patient have a good line?"

"Yes, Dr. Arty, the IV line was just placed in this morning," one of the interns informed me.

"If the patient hasn't received any medications yet, give him five milligrams of epinephrine and continue with the compressions," I said, looking at the EKG monitor.

So far, my only thought had been the cardiac arrest protocol—doing the right things to hopefully save a life. As members of the code team, the doctors, nurses, and respiratory personnel were so used to handling cardiac arrests that it was practically second nature.

"Hold compressions," I ordered. "Is there a pulse?"

"No pulse."

From my point of view at the foot of the bed, all I could see was an amputated right leg and a chin with an oxygen mask covering the area where the patient's mouth and nose should be. Above that was a hand making sure that the mask's seal was tight.

"Give the patient one milligram of atropine and continue with the compressions," I replied. While I was setting up the endotracheal tube in order to intubate the patient, the anesthesiologist finally showed up with the respiratory therapist in tow.

"Here's the chart, Dr. Arty," a nurse said and placed it in my hand. I quickly glanced through the admissions form to find the patient's identity and diagnosis.

I felt a tightening in my chest as my eyes read the patient's name. Peter Fields, a sixty-seven-year-old veteran with peripheral vascular disease and diabetes. Peter Fields, the first war veteran I ever befriended. *What was he doing coding on the ninth floor of the Brooklyn Veterans Administration Hospital? Lord, I didn't even know he was admitted,* I thought.

The last time I spoke to him, he was home planning a move to California. That was three weeks ago. Today, he is fighting for his life.

As these thoughts ran through my mind, my eyes searched the face of the man under the oxygen mask in hopes that this patient was not Peter. But the weak chin, sunken pale face, thinning white hair, and amputated right leg left me no hope to cling to. I quickly looked over at the EKG monitor and saw the flat line daring me to do something.

"Another five milligrams of epinephrine," I said, "and continue with the compressions."

So far the prognosis didn't look good. We were at least seven minutes into the code, and the only bleep on the EKG monitor was the one caused by the compressions on Peter's chest. I already knew he had very poor circulation since our first meeting had resulted in the amputation of his right leg. In less time than it takes to think, memories of that first meeting entered my thoughts.

———

It was two years ago, and I was a medical intern on call at the Brooklyn VA Hospital.

I first met Peter in a poorly lit, large multi-bedded room with windows looking out toward the Verrazano Bridge. He was sitting next to the bed in a chair with tears rolling down both his cheeks. As he noticed me entering the room, he quickly wiped his face with the back of his hand.

"About time you got here, Doc! What's a fellow gotta do to see a doctor around here? I've been sitting here for maybe two hours!" he yelled at me.

"I'm sorry you had to wait, sir, but I had other patients to see before you," I replied.

"Yeah, well, it's always the same here. Whenever you get admitted, you have to wait maybe two or three hours before seeing a doctor. At least some things never change," he said.

Yes, I thought, *some things never change—like doing your best to remain civil while a patient vents their frustrations on you.* "My name is Dr. Arty," I said. "I'll be your doctor during your hospitalization. I came by to speak to you and examine you."

"Dr. Arty, huh?" he replied. "Well, Arty, I hope you know what you're doing. Every time I come in here, I get some hotshot that speaks in that doctor mumbo jumbo talk that I can hardly understand. Worst of all, they don't even listen to me when I try to say something. Well, at least you speak English. That's a good start!"

"Mr. Fields," I said, "I've read in the emergency room notes that you had a leg pain that is now interfering with the way you walk. Could you tell me a little more about it?"

"Tell you about it? Sure. That's why I'm here. For a couple of months now, I've been having a pain down my right leg. It only gets real bad when I walk, and when I stop walking, it feels a lot better. I used to try to walk through it, but it's getting worse."

After examining Mr. Fields and finding no pulse below his right knee, I decided to consult with the surgical service.

"Sir, I think I will need to speak to the vascular surgeons about the problem. They may be able to help you better than I can."

He looked anxious. "What the hell are you saying, Doc? You think I'll need surgery?" he asked me.

"I'm not saying that you will need surgery. That's not my decision to make. All I'm saying, Mr. Fields, is that your problem needs surgical consultation."

"Well, what the hell are you saying?" he barked at me. "Are you a doctor, or what? Don't play games with me. If I need surgery, just let me know!"

As he finished speaking, his eyes looked away from me. He turned his chair and gave me his back. Looking at his frail shoulders, it seemed to me as if the chair had swallowed him. He somehow appeared much smaller than when I first entered the room.

"Mr. Fields, can I help you with anything?" I asked.

"No, kid. You've done enough. Just leave me in peace," he replied. From the tone of his voice, I could tell he was near tears, but he was not going to give me the chance to comfort him. On my way out of the room, I remembered hearing him crying.

———

"How long have we been in this code?" I asked.

"Ten minutes, Dr. Arty," the supervising nurse answered. "Are you thinking of terminating the code?"

"No! Give him another EPI and continue with the compressions." I watched as the anesthesiologist bent Peter's head back to tape the endotracheal tube around his mouth. Looking at Peter's frail old body taking on all this punishment, I remembered meeting Peter again after his leg amputation.

———

He had been transferred to the surgical vascular service the day after I met him. A week of tests confirmed his poor circulation and resulted in an amputation of his right leg below the knee. One afternoon, on one of those too few occasions when I managed to get my work done early, I decided to pay him a visit. Going down the elevator from the ninth floor, I pressed the button to the fourth floor. When the elevator stopped at my floor, I made a right and walked down the corridor to the nurses' station, where I found one of the surgical floor nurses busy preparing to give out medications.

"What room is Mr. Peter Fields in?" I asked.

"Room six. Third door down the hall to your left."

"Thank you," I replied. I went to the four-bed room and found Peter lying in the first bed by the door, reading a magazine with his leg under some covers. "Hello, Mr. Fields! How are you feeling?" I asked.

He slowly raised his head, placed his paper on the bed, and, with a wide grin, surprised me by inviting me to sit down on the chair next to his bed. "Hey, Arty, how are you doing? Boy, where've you been? I thought you forgot about me. You know, I knew I would need to have an operation, and I know you thought so too. Why didn't you just come out straight and tell me?" he asked.

"Mr. Fields, I didn't know for certain that you needed an operation. I was hoping that the surgeons could have done something for you without resorting to surgery, but I guess the tests showed the extent of the damage to your leg. I'm sorry," I said.

"Arty, don't be sorry. You did what was expected of you. Anyway, thanks for the visit."

We chatted for a while, and as I was about to leave, he asked, "Could you do me a favor?"

"Depends on what it is," I answered.

He smiled at my response. "You work at Kings County Hospital, don't you?"

"Yes, why?" I replied.

"Well, my wife is there, and she's lying in a bed not knowing how I am 'cause I can't visit her. You see, she's got bad circulation like me, and the doctors were talking about having to cut her leg off too. I don't know what's happening to her. Would you check on her for me if it ain't out of your way?"

It was a pretty personal request. *Why doesn't one of his friends or family members tell him what is happening with his wife?* I thought.

As if to answer me, he continued. "Arty, my wife is all I got. All we've got is each other. We don't have any kids, and most of our friends have either died or live out of state. Arty, you just don't know," he said. I quietly sat in the chair and listened to his story. Slowly, tears carved their way down his cheeks, and his voice broke into a whisper, "Arty, I've been so lonely without her…worrying about her. I love her so much. Please, just go check on her. Oh! Man. I don't mean to cry in front of you. It just hurts so much inside. When you see her tell her that I love her."

"Hold compressions and check for a pulse. Are you hearing breath sounds yet?" I asked.

"Yeah!" the anesthesiologist replied after successfully intubating Peter. "All right, nurse, hang some dopamine, and let's get a blood gas. Give him another five milligrams EPI," I said.

Come on, Peter, fight! I mentally shouted at him, all the while hoping that his heart would respond to the medication.

Since I lived two blocks away from Kings County Hospital at the time, it was not a problem to check in on his wife. The following Saturday afternoon, I found her in a room on the surgical service at the hospital, and from the description given to me by Peter, I was able to recognize her easily. She was a large-framed woman with curly graying blond hair. She was resting on her bed reading a tabloid newspaper. She seemed oblivious to her surroundings.

I quietly approached her and introduced myself. "Good afternoon, ma'am. How are you doing today?"

She looked up at me, obviously startled, but quickly recovered and replied with a smile, "I'm fine, thanks. Do I know you?"

"No, ma'am, you don't. My name is Dr. Arty, and I'm one of the doctors looking after your husband, Mr. Fields. He wanted me to stop by and see how you were doing because he hadn't heard from you. He wants you to know that he's doing okay."

She looked at me as if the world had stopped turning. It seemed like she was playing my words in her mind again and again. After a couple of seconds, she burst out, "Thank God, he's all right! Thank you for coming…You don't know what this means to me! I've been so worried about him! Thank you…thank you so much!" Then, like her husband, she began to cry quietly.

I looked around and gratefully found a box of tissues.

"You can't know what this means to me," she said after a couple of minutes of trying to stop crying. "We've been married for forty years, and we've seldom ever been apart. All we have is each other, and there just hasn't been a way for me to find out how he's been. He used to come and visit a couple of weeks ago, but then told me that he was going to check into the hospital for some tests. Since then I haven't heard from him. I know that he is at the VA, but it was breaking my heart not to know how he was. No one here seemed to be able to help me. Is he really okay?"

"Yes, ma'am, he's fine. He wanted me to tell you not to worry about him, that all is well. He also wanted me to let you know how much he loves and misses you."

"Dr. Arty, the intravenous line stopped working, and there's no access for the dopamine," a nurse shouted toward me, bringing me back to the hospital room where Peter was dying. This was bad news. The Coronary Care Unit resident and I immediately attempted to gain access using other major veins in his body. "Everyone hold compressions and check for a pulse," I ordered. We were not able to feel a pulse. "Continue with compressions, and give him another five milligrams of epinephrine. Keep giving him oxygen. Make sure the air is getting in," I told the anesthesiologist at the head of the bed. By this time, a medical student came in with the results of the blood gas showing that Peter's body was becoming depleted of oxygen. "I hope you've been getting those breaths in," I said to the respiratory therapist. "I'm doing all I can, Doc," he replied.

My mind traveled back to seeing Peter last year in the VA cafeteria.

I was busy making small talk with one of the pharmacists in the hospital when I heard the sound of a distinct raspy voice, saying, "Come on, buddy, you gonna stand there all day?" I turned around to see Peter in a wheelchair, trying to maneuver himself from behind several patrons who were slowly looking for seats. He managed to find a table reserved for handicapped veterans without spilling the tray of food he was carrying on his lap. I abruptly ended the conversation I was engaged in and went to greet Peter. "Mr. Fields, how are you? I haven't seen you in maybe a year and a half. How have you been?" I asked.

"Hey, look at that. It's Arty, my favorite doc. How the hell are you, man? You look like you gained a little weight. Life must be easier since you're not an intern anymore."

"Well, life is certainly different nowadays. Less running around, but more responsibilities," I replied. "Hey, Mr. Fields, how is Mrs. Fields doing?"

"She may be doing better than me, Arty. She passed away nine months ago," he said while playing with his food. "A heart attack is what killed her."

I didn't know what to say. Normally, the appropriate thing to do would have been to say, "I'm sorry," but I didn't want to sound mechanical. I wound up not saying anything for a while and just sat across the small table with Peter sharing the moment. Finally, I said, "I didn't know Mr. Fields…I'm sorry."

"Of course you didn't know Arty. How could you? And would you please stop calling me Mr. Fields? Call me Pete. Anyway, she died mercifully in her sleep, and she had a beautiful funeral, as funerals go."

After a while, he said, "I tell you, Arty, I miss her more than I miss my leg. You know somethin'? You never really know how much you miss someone until they're no longer there. But the thought that she's in a much better place helps me get through many nights. The other night, I woke up, and the realization that I was not going to see her ever again in this life…that I'll only be able to hear her voice again in my memories hit me like a ton of bricks. If I hadn't gotten a grip on myself, I think I would have tried to jump out of my window 'cause the weight of her absence was so heavy…so unbearable." And with a sigh, he said, "She was my anchor to reality. I feel so unplugged from life."

Peter paused after sharing his pain with me, and I was grateful for the pause. Somehow, for a moment, I sensed a measure of his crushing heartache and wondered how he bore it. After some time spent looking at the table, Peter said, "Hey, Arty, we've been meeting here at the hospital these last couple of years…Why don't you visit me? Don't you doctors make house calls anymore?"

I was surprised by his invitation. I had never thought about visiting Peter at his home. Since I was not yet an attending doctor, I was not making "house calls" to patients' homes, and in any event, I had not yet met any attending doctors who did make house calls. I thought that was a thing of the past. But I was still curious to know how Peter lived his life.

———◦◦◦◦◦———

"Dr. Arty, the patient is not responding," a loud voice said, shaking me out of my thoughts.

"Get some sodium bicarb in him," I replied. I felt a lump in my throat as I said it, fully aware of Peter's fight for his life. Like any doctor, I didn't want to lose a patient, but Peter was someone who opened the door of his world and invited me in.

———◦◦◦◦◦———

"Come on in, Arty. Come on in," Peter greeted me with a familiar grin that showed the wrinkles on his face, and I entered through his apartment door. "*Mi casa es su casa.*" So you do make house calls. I don't get many visitors except for that woman who comes in to check up on me every two days. Hey, Arty, my man… you wanna beer?"

In his excitement, Peter didn't seem to take any breaths as the words ran out of his mouth. He expertly maneuvered his wheelchair as he ushered me into his small one-bedroom apartment facing Flatbush Avenue in Brooklyn. I could hear the honking of car horns and the voices of children playing outside his window. I saw a small wooden cabinet to my left, which I later discovered contained what Peter considered to be the "only good films around," including his *Rambo* and *Die Hard* collections.

In the living room, pictures of Peter and his wife were placed everywhere.

Peter had pictures on his small circular coffee table; on top of the television, which sat across from an old tan sofa still covered with clear plastic; on the walls; and even on the dusty windowsills. Each picture was neatly placed in a wooden or metallic frame and strategically positioned to be seen from almost any corner of the room. The pictures told a beautiful story of many years of sharing a life with a partner. Peter took the time to explain to me when and where each picture was taken. With each picture, Peter's face seemed to melt as he emotionally entered the photograph. I saw Peter and his wife in the deserts of several Midwestern states. I saw pictures taken on snowy mountains, on beaches, with friends; pictures of old cars from the 1950s, '60s, and '70s. They were filled with smiles and happiness. They spoke of one man's yesterdays that would never be again and were bittersweet because of it. Each picture in its respected frame seemed to form a physical padding of protection from the brutal and lonely reality of Peter's present.

I was touched by Peter's hospitality that afternoon. He tried his best to make me feel as comfortable as possible. As I sat with the plastic-covered sofa stubbornly holding on to the bottom of my pants, the sound of the cars outside his first floor apartment along with the children's voices slowly faded while Peter discussed his favorite movies…

⸻

"Okay, we've got something on the monitor," the nurse said jubilantly.

"Hand me the defibrillator pads…I want immediate defibrillation," I shouted when I noticed the rhythm on the monitor and knew that we still did not have a pulse. "Hold compressions and clear the area!" I quickly placed the two electrical pads on Peter's thin chest, now bruised from our attempts to keep him alive. As his body danced with the electricity, I wondered for a moment if this was something Peter would have wanted.

⸻

"Never had a headache…know what I mean?" Peter asked me.

"Okay, so what about it?" I asked. I was glued to Peter's plastic-covered sofa opposite the television during my second "house call." He repeated himself, this time slowly as if he was worried that I couldn't understand the English language. "She never…ever…

had…a…headache. Do you understand what I'm saying, Arty? That's how it was with us. I would hear other guys talk about how their wives would get headaches every once in a while and couldn't… you know…be with them."

At that point, Peter was speaking hesitantly, carefully choosing each word in order to discuss this sensitive subject. For my part, I was honored that he would open up to me in this way. "Arty, my wife would always be there for me. In forty years of marriage, she never once told me she had a headache," Peter said, his voice now a little bit louder than a whisper. "And this may sound even harder to believe, but we hardly ever fought. Oh, sure we had disagreements, but in all that time, Arty, I can't remember us having any serious arguments. See, we made this covenant with one another like in the Bible and agreed never to go to bed angry. We were in it for the long haul. Once she left her parents' house, she never went back. We would talk about everything. Arty man, you just don't know. She made living easy. She made life easy for me."

"Dr. Arty, I think I have a pulse," the medical student said. I looked at the monitor and felt satisfied when I saw the sinus rhythm smiling back at me.

"All right, we have sinus rhythm…Good work, people…Now let's get him to the ICU," I said.

We worked in unison as we moved Peter from his hospital bed onto the stretcher waiting for him outside his room. Ironically, that same stretcher would have escorted him to the morgue if circumstances were different. We rushed Peter toward the elevator to get to the ICU on the fourth floor as soon as possible in order to place him on a respirator.

I could tell by the tone of the voices around me that everyone was happy we were able to get a pulse going. It meant that we saved a life, and that is what we were trained to do. But I also wondered if Peter would have been as happy with our success as we were. I contemplated that question on my way home that evening, struggling between my duties as a physician and what I knew of Peter. I couldn't see the dignity and respect for life in that long dragged-out code. On the other hand, I didn't have it in me to stand by as a passive witness to Peter's passing. That was not part of my medical training.

My mental and emotional torment ended when I returned to work the following day and discovered that Peter had coded again during the night and was not able to be resuscitated. To be honest, I was not surprised by that discovery. I knew deep down in that place where everyone comes to believe, that Peter would not leave the hospital in his mortal frame. It was only a matter of time. But I was surprised by my emotional response. I felt so absolutely relieved! It was as if an elephant had been lifted off my chest. *No more lingering*, I thought. His body didn't have to linger on in a facsimile of life. I remembered the man who after such soul-shattering losses still had such life shining behind his smile.

———

"Arty! Where in the name of all that's holy did you learn to drive? I'm going to catch a case of whiplash! Can you take it easy on the brake?" Peter's raspy voice began to sound worse than nails scraping against a dull blackboard. I was getting irritated after having volunteered to take Peter to "run a quick errand not too far from here" and having to suffer through his incessant criticism of my driving. To make matters worse, I suspected that he was exaggerating his head and neck bobbing motions every time I came to a full stop. It was a hot summer afternoon in Brooklyn, and traffic on Flatbush Avenue was at a standstill. To make matters worse, Peter's lips refused to stop flapping long enough for me to get a moment of silence and form a clear idea about how we were going to get out of this traffic jam. Thankfully, my car's air conditioner was working.

"Arty man, I told you we should've taken Nostrand Avenue, but nooo…you said you knew better…Flatbush Avenue was better you said…Man, I'm gonna die here, and you gonna grow old sitting in this car," he continued. I almost laughed out loud because I clearly recalled that it was him who made those suggestions. My frown stretched into a little smirk as I contemplated the possibility that Peter might be trying to reward me with blame for agreeing to do a favor for him. "Pete...you must be losing your mind. It was you who said to take Flatbush Avenue," I replied, trying to sound more annoyed than I was.

Peter must have picked up the annoyance in my voice and surprisingly stayed quiet for several long minutes. I decided not to break the silence.

Finally, he said, "Let me outta here, Arty. I'm gonna walk home."

"You mean you're going to hop home!" I replied. "Listen, Pete, we're too far away for me to let you go out of this car with your one-leg self. Just let me try to get us out of here."

"Arty, what did you say? Tell me I didn't just hear you say I can't get home on my own." As his voice filled with anger, he said, "I don't give a rat's ass what you think, Arty. Just let me get my crutch! Walk, hop, skip, crawl, I'm outta this car." Peter's voice sounded serious enough, but I didn't want him having to walk with his crutches the several blocks it would have taken to return to his apartment building.

"Okay, Pete...listen. I'm sure you can get home on your own, but I'd really prefer that you let me take you back home. It's really hot out there." Peter stayed quiet for several minutes and then suddenly broke into laughter. "Man, are you kiddin'? I was just bustin' your chops...I ain't walking out there in that heat. I'm no fool. Of course, you gonna take me home." I sat in the car next to Peter, watching him laugh uncontrollably, and I found myself laughing with him.

I went to find out who the medical senior was during the night but unfortunately discovered that the senior had already gone home. Normally, when a patient dies, it falls to the medical senior on call or the patient's attending physician to contact the family, but in all the time I had known Peter, I never met any family member other than his wife. Nor had he mentioned the name of another friend, or at least one who was alive.

Peter died that night, and there was no one to come and claim his body. The following day, I left the VA hospital to begin my next rotation at Kings County Hospital.

I write about Peter today to let him breathe again, to let the love he shared with his wife of forty years be as fresh today as when they were both alive. By opening up the door of his life to me and inviting me in, he gave me the best of what he had. It may sound simple and trite, but our time together was of the simplest and purest quality, and I guess I wanted a little more.

My thoughts occasionally rest on the memory of Peter, and when they do, I find myself smiling.

I Don't Know

I'm sitting in a poorly lit waiting room with my lawyer to my right, waiting to answer questions about a tragic event that took place in a facility that I was, by title, responsible for. The interview had already been set back by a half hour, and now we have been waiting for an additional forty minutes. I try to look calm, examining a showcase decorated with several awards for outstanding police activity. My eyes move to a photograph of the New York skyline during the 1970s, and our eyes meet as my lawyer makes a comment about the photograph. I suspect he is trying to put me at ease, and I appreciate it, but there are only so many comments we can make about a photograph while I wait to be interrogated about something I had nothing to do with.

I received a subpoena about a week ago indicating that I needed to be at this interview. I didn't know what the legal consequences were if I didn't attend, nor did I want to know. Based on some recent negative experiences that I have had with lawyers, their world is not a place I feel comfortable living in. My intention was to make this interview as short as possible.

After a few more minutes of looking around the room, a well-dressed, small-framed man walks in, introduces himself, and apologizes for keeping us waiting. He informs us that he is one of the lawyers who will be participating in the interview process and that it won't be too much longer. He appreciates our patience. He then disappears, and I go back to examining the New York skyline, remembering visits to the World Trade Center Towers with my mother and sister when we were children. After another fifteen minutes, the man returns, apologizes again, and escorts us into an elevator.

We step out of the elevator into a room lined with old bookcases storing volumes of books. I detect the scent of old pages in the room, and there aren't any windows in this little area. I'm thinking that this is to prevent me from being distracted from the questions that will be posed to me.

At the center of the room is a long rectangular table with three seats on each of the ends. Eventually, a man and a woman enter the room, and we are introduced. They are also lawyers. The one who takes the center seat across from me is quiet. He tells me that he will be listening to my answers and interrupting just to clarify some points. He is a tall, bald Caucasian, most likely in his early fifties, with a face that seems to give a hint of sympathy but not much more. The woman to his right seems emotionally distant from me and wears a pasted-on smile. In that place deep inside that helps us navigate our way around emotional land mines, I sense that this is all intentional. I don't want to be here, and even my lawyer's reassuring presence doesn't make me feel like staying here one moment longer than needed.

Our greeter sits to their left and is exceptionally friendly, loosening his tie and offering me a cup of water before my interview begins. His voice and demeanor are calming, trying to put me at ease. He is the "good cop" to the woman lawyer's "bad cop." Even before we begin, the "good cop" takes out a small tape recorder to get my responses on record. That doesn't do much to alleviate my anxiety.

He explains to me that this interview is an attempt to understand the truth of how a facility operates. I have heard it said that truth, like beauty, is in the eye of the beholder, so I am left wondering which truth they want to hear. Is it the truth from my perspective or theirs? I really don't know.

I understand that sometimes, titular heads have to take the fall for things done on their watch, but I had been removed from any authoritative role for months prior to the event. I was systematically and purposefully left blind and deaf to the changes taking place in the department that might have contributed to this tragedy. And then I was fired. So why is my name even being connected with this? I don't know.

While growing up, I was often encouraged to "say what you mean and mean what you say," and I've tried to adhere to that as much as possible while living this life. I often take the time to think about my response before it comes out of my mouth, so at times I noticeably pause before answering a question. In preparation for this interview, I was instructed not to speculate or guess when responding to questions. If I absolutely didn't know the answer to a question, the only answer is to be "I don't know." Even if I think I know the answer, if I am not absolutely sure of the answer, my response is to be "I don't know." I was also informed that I am not the focus of the investigation and that my role is to provide a background for the investigation. My interrogation is apparently to be conducted in a "friendly" manner. But the word *friendly*, like beauty and truth, is also in the eye of the beholder.

The "good cop" unbuttons and rolls up his shirtsleeves to indicate that we are about to begin. I suddenly notice how hot the room is and take off my jacket. I also notice a small tear on the left sleeve of my shirt and hope no one else does. With a gentle voice and a smile, good cop asks me to begin by telling them about my background and how I came to my present position of employment. That seems benign enough, and after all, I think the easiest thing for people to do is to talk about themselves. How difficult can that be? I begin to discuss where I went to school and completed my residencies, but as my lips move and I listen to myself speak, I keep thinking that they already know this information. I know for a fact that they have secured my employment record and have copies of all my evaluations. So what is really behind this question? I don't know. Have they already evaluated me and concluded that I was not adequate for the position? Are they looking for evidence to support my dismissal? I don't know.

Sitting at this table, across from these three lawyers, I feel as if I have fallen into a world of words where each word takes on a hue that can either work for me or against me, or whatever I say can be twisted to reflect the thoughts of my interrogators. I am acutely aware of every word coming out of my mouth and how they are joining together to create the sentences that hopefully reflect clear thoughts. In this lawyer's world, so unlike the doctor's world, what you mean is easily susceptible to manipulation even if you think you know what you mean.

With each question I am asked, I feel the circle of questions tightening around me and the "friendly" nature of our interaction becoming less and less "friendly." It is not exactly hostile, but it has gone beyond friendly business. Somewhere along the way, from asking about my background to explaining my job responsibilities,

I am beginning to feel more and more that I am being considered responsible for something.

"Were you in charge at the time of the event? If not, when were you in charge? What were your responsibilities? What were the circumstances like when you were in charge? What do you know about this employee? And what about that employee? Have you heard anything about this individual that would concern you? Why exactly were you fired? Walk us through the process of how things normally take place."

I'm trying to answer to the best of my recollection about the microscopic aspects of an operation in which I held a macroscopic role. I am reluctant to say, "I don't know," repeatedly about some of the day-to-day aspects of the operations. It is making me look bad, as if I didn't know my own facility.

As if reading my anxiety, the female bad cop lawyer interjects, "C'mon, Doc, you mean to tell me that you were the head of this place for the past four years and you don't know about the people working for you?" I consider her question and remember that I had heard rumors having to do with some of the individuals the lawyer has mentioned, but they were only rumors. How can I put on record rumors that I am not able to substantiate? Once again, I have to say, "I don't know."

In a show of exasperation and without warning, the "bad cop" lawyer whips out a document that I had apparently signed several months ago. She places it in front of me. She asks, "Do you remember this document? Didn't you sign this document several months ago? Isn't that your signature? Can you tell me why you had this policy generated? How was it distributed?"

I ask to examine the document. It is undeniably my signature. I need a few minutes to read the document, process it, and recall the circumstances surrounding its birth. Her facial expression and body language do not seem to want to give me that opportunity. The "good cop" is silent, and the quiet one in the middle is looking intensely at me. I understand that this is the "spike," the "in your face" moment that is supposed to surprise me and cause me to be more imbalanced than I already am. This is no longer a "friendly" interview.

My job was to approve of the various policies and procedures that were being generated by my department. In the rush of questions being asked of me, I couldn't recall the exact reason for this particular policy but knew that it was distributed throughout the facility. How it was distributed was left up to our clinical educator. At the time, I was told that it was distributed, but I was not present when the distribution took place. And of course I am under oath, so all that I am saying can later be brought up for cross-examination. Once again, I answer what I am sure of, and the rest goes into the "I don't know" box.

After an hour and a half of this kind of questioning, I am told that they have no other questions. They appreciate my coming down to clarify things. Clarify what? I don't know. I am given an opportunity to add anything else that would help with their investigation. At this point, I'm not really sure what they are investigating. The female lawyer "bad cop" walks us out of the foyer with the same fixed smile she greeted us with, and we spend a few awkward moments making polite conversation while waiting for the elevator to come and mercifully take me away. I hate this moment; I'm feeling as if I am being kicked out of the place more than being escorted out. I don't know if my responses were satisfactory or appropriate.

I hold my breath until the elevator reaches the lobby. I can't remember if I shook "bad cop's" hand or just said good-bye. We exit the building, and I exhale. My lawyer tells me I did fine, and he was happy to learn how I handle questions under pressure. For my part, I'm not sure what I had just gone through. Was I being accused of something? Was I defending myself? It sure felt that way.

Did I answer appropriately? Why was I fired? Am I in trouble? I don't know.

The Penguins of Manhattan Beach

The waves are angry today. They rush at the beach like walls of water and furiously disperse into bubbling white foam, then scurry back into the sea. There is no other place I would rather be today than at this beach, swimming in the ocean with my father.

It's a beautiful September afternoon, one of the last warm days of the summer. This is the third time I have been to the beach this summer, and I can't recall experiencing a day like this one. The sun is bright, and there are a few wispy clouds floating almost too high in the sky to be seen. The absence of clouds allows me to see the sky in all its vastness. I feel the sun's warm rays gently kissing my shoulders and back. The waves are strong, pushing our bodies in toward the shore, and pulling us back into the ocean. The water is not as clear as I would like it to be, but then again it's not as dark as it could be. The saltiness of the sea lingers in my mouth and tickles my nostrils every time I dunk my head in the water. Several beaches in New York have already closed, and there aren't too many visitors on this beach. The lifeguards packed up and left at least two weeks ago.

It seems that my father and I, along with the few who came out on this Monday afternoon, are trying to squeeze the last drops of summer from the sun before the cool temperatures of the fall chase us away.

My father, whom I have called PaAtie for as long as I can remember, had insisted that I bring him to the beach a final time before the summer ended. His rationale was that the number three is the trinity, the number for completion, and we had only been in the ocean twice before. With a third bath in the salty ocean water, he believed he would get a total cleansing, rejuvenation, and healing for his tired muscles and bones. Afterward, his intention is to sleep through the night with the salt on his skin. That would complete his self-imposed treatment. Although I found his ideas peculiar, I of course obliged. I would enjoy spending the afternoon with him.

Since I was fired from my job two months ago, I've been trying to catch up on the things most important in my life. I've also struggled with feelings of anger and hurt over my dismissal, but there is a sense of liberation, as if chains have fallen from my ankles and wrists and I am free to fly. I chose to catch up on my relationship with my father, get to know him a little more, and maybe hear him laugh a little louder. Free moments like these have been rare for me, and I want to savor every second of them.

Our afternoon on the beach started out with my father coming to a startling realization as I was changing into my swimming trunks.

"Oh! I can't believe I forgot my swimming trunks."

"Well, I guess you won't be able to swim," I responded.

After a moment, he asked, "What's that guy wearing? It looks like underwear."

A thin-framed man was walking on the beach, wearing black Speedo swim briefs.

"That's not underwear. Those are swimming shorts," I said.

"No. That's underwear. And I have black underwear on me just like that."

"PaAtie, that's his swimming gear. That's not his underwear."

"Well, it looks like underwear from here. I think it's his underwear. If he can wear his underwear at the beach, I can do the same."

"PaAtie, that's not his underwear."

I obviously wasn't going to convince him that the thin man was wearing black Speedos, and in any event, my father was already stripped down to his black Fruit of the Looms. Thankfully, Manhattan Beach was not crowded on this Monday afternoon, so I didn't think anyone was going to scrutinize the band around his waist, and even if they did, I reasoned with myself that he wasn't breaking any laws.

I couldn't help but examine the body of the man from whose loins I came as he approached the ocean in his black underwear. As I looked at my father, I wondered if my body was destined to look like his when I reached my late '70s. Was I to be shorter, rounder, and softer? When I was a child, I used to look at his hands and fingers and wondered if mine would look like his. I even remembered him doing a handstand in the house one afternoon. I wanted to be able to be as strong and able as he was. But now, I'm becoming a bit concerned about what my body may look like in the not-so-distant future. While thinking about this, it occurred to me that it wouldn't be so bad as long as I had his *"joie de vivre,"* his joy of life.

I was the first to jump into the ocean and feel the water's coolness against my skin. It gave my whole body a jolt. I laughed loudly as I dove into the water and encouraged my father to jump in and join me. He followed, not wanting to look skittish. He surprised me by jumping in and popped up with a grin as wide as mine across his face.

Now we are both in the ocean, splashing and enjoying the sensation of being nearly weightless in the water.

I ask my father if he knows how to swim different strokes, and he answers, "Of course. I grew up in Haiti, near the ocean. Every boy I grew up with knew how to swim several different ways."

"Can you show me what you know?"

And he shows me how he does the backstroke, the breaststroke, and the crawl. Each style looks exactly the same to me, but I nod and say, "Yeah, I see what you mean."

I swim a little farther out toward the open sea and motion for him to follow me, saying that the water is warmer farther out. He refuses with a warning, "Sometimes a wave can come in and take you out to sea, and then you may develop a cramp and can't swim back. That can be the end of you. *Lame pa gen plezantri*" (The ocean is no joke).

"Okay, I won't go out too far," I respond. "And don't drink any of this seawater. I don't trust it."

I swim for the next half hour and watch my father turn away from the ocean so the waves can directly hit his lower back. With each wave that massages his back, he breathes out *"Li bon"* (That's good). At one point, he returns to the water's edge and lies down on the sand so the waves can cover him like a blanket. Upon standing, he coughs up the water that he nearly drank and once again exhales, *"Li bon."*

Later we take a break from swimming, and I join him sitting on the sand. The sand feels comfortably warm against our skin, and we sit for a moment in silence, looking at the seagulls and other beachgoers on this sunny afternoon. Our legs are taking on a darker shade of brown. My father notices a woman wearing a thong bikini and comments on how liberal America is.

"*Moun isi fou*. People here are crazy. People do what they want here, and no one can say anything to them. That's the beauty of this country. You're free to live your life. Look at her. She's naked on the beach, and no one has a problem with that!"

It occurs to me that although we are and will always be father and son, the nuances of our relationship have changed. I came out here to enjoy being with my father, and I am realizing that we have come to a new place in understanding how our relationship has changed. The language we used while I was growing up seems insufficient now, and we are finding a new one to bridge the distance between us. Now we speak freely about women, sex, money, and other matters that we had never discussed in the past. He compares life in America with that in Haiti and makes comments that have us both laughing.

After a silence, we look at the noisy seagulls landing on the beach and on top of the metal baskets of garbage. We comment on how aggressive they seem, trying to open plastic bags with their beaks. Some even try to get near us, possibly being used to getting fed by beachgoers.

"Look at these birds. They are so much more aggressive than the ones in Haiti. They just come right up to you…They have no respect," he says to me.

"Nope, they sure don't. You ready to get back in the water?"

"What? What do you think…I'm a fish? I came for a bath, and I got what I came for. Do you know how long we were in the water?"

"PaAtie, it's only been an hour. Besides, the sun is still out, and we're having a good time. C'mon, let's get back in the water."

"Okay. But I'm not sleeping out here."

Once again, we plunge into the ocean like two penguins jumping off a glacier. I can tell he is having a good time. And so am I. I swim around my father, showing off my own limited swimming abilities while again encouraging him to go a little farther out with me. He stands up in the water and watches a man who is jogging back and forth along the beach. My father loves to people watch, and he is doing it now from this new vantage point. He points to an old man who is vigorously flailing his arms around before doing some jumping jacks.

"See, Pierre, that's what I do every morning. That's what keeps me looking so good."

As my father is speaking, we hear a faint voice calling out in our direction and turn to see a dark hat with a head underneath bobbing out from the surface of the water a distance away. It looks like a woman, and she seems to be waving at us. I wave back, and she keeps waving. She appears to be near some rocks.

I turn back to my father, and he points to a young woman sunbathing on the beach.

"That girl has to be sad. She probably broke up with her boyfriend. Why else would she be here by herself looking so sad?"

I'm impressed that he is able to see her face behind her sunglasses considering how far away she is.

The desperate cry of a woman's voice interrupts our conversation. We turn and see the same woman we saw before under the dark hat waving at me.

"Hi!" I shout to her. "Are you okay?"

She keeps waving without speaking. Now others on the beach are staring in her direction. But they are just standing and looking. *Her relatives must be somewhere on the beach*, I think, but no one approaches her.

"PaAtie, I'm going over there to see what is going on with this woman. I'll be back. Just wait for me here."

My father doesn't say anything but keeps looking at the woman waving her arm in the water.

I start swimming toward her, mindful of the increasing depth of the water. In spite of all my showboating in front of my father, I'm not really a good swimmer. A few feet away from the woman, I notice how elderly and tired her face looks. I also realize what has happened to her. The waves in this area, next to the rocks are very strong. Much stronger than where my father and I were swimming. They come, hit the rocks, and return to the sea, carrying with them whatever is in their grasp. She has been trying to swim back to the shore, but the current holds her like a prisoner.

I stop swimming to try to feel the ocean floor, and I can barely touch it. I decide to walk to her and pull her back to shore, concerned about being pulled out to sea with her. I thank God I had told my father to wait for me. I would hate to have to worry about pulling both him and this woman if he had come out here with me. A moment after being comforted by that thought, I look up and see my father approaching me. There is no stopping him. He's coming to help.

Approaching her slowly, I see how pale she looks. *How long has she been out here, treading water?* I wonder. I have to reach her and bring her in before we all fall victim to these waves. She reaches out to me with her right arm. I grab hold of it, feeling the waves pushing me out, away from the beach. I use my feet to anchor me on the ocean floor and pull us toward the rocks, where I'm hoping to grab and hold the side of one. My father manages to maneuver himself around her, reaches for her left arm, and holds it. Now we are a human chain, with the waves pushing against us. We begin to move slowly toward the rocks. While walking almost on my toes, I am thinking about my father, hoping not to lose him to the same fate he warned me about earlier. *Lame pa gen plezantri*, and we are resisting being swept out to sea.

A few curious observers stand on top of other rocks and watch the drama play in front of them without offering assistance. When we finally make our way to shallow waters, we let go of the woman's arms. She walks out of the water shaking and says, "Thank you. Thank you," with a smile that highlights what seems to be dentures ready to fall out of her mouth and an accent that sounds very Eastern European. With an unsteady gait, she slowly walks away from us and heads toward the area of the beach where her belongings are waiting.

After losing sight of her, we sit down again on the sand, to talk about what just took place.

"PaAtie…I thought you would have stayed where you were and waited for me. I could have lost you out there. The waves could have carried you away."

"She could have died if we hadn't come along. She shouldn't have been out there on her own. Where is her family? People just do things on their own in this country. Everyone is so independent," he responds.

"I think she would have been lost out there. I can't believe that people just stood there watching and didn't try to help us. I thought that some of these folks on the beach were her family."

With a sigh, he acknowledges and agrees with me. We both look at the folks on the beach who have already returned to whatever they were doing.

"You saved her life, PaAtie. You know that, right?"

He doesn't say anything but looks out into the ocean.

A few minutes later, he turns, looks at me, and says, *"Papa ou toujou gwo neg"* (Your father is still a strong man).

"Yeah, I guess he still is," I say in response.

God Is Good
(Bondye Bon)

Every so often, a situation presents itself that tests the very foundation of your belief system and removes every pretense. You find yourself stripped of every self-imposed fantasy of security, leaving only your core—no friends, parents, or family, just you. Your response reveals who you are…what you are. You may even discover that you are not who you thought you were and life, with all its meaning, is redefined. This is the crossing over, the elementary experience of living. It is the rite of passage from childhood fantasies to the reality of adulthood.

When do we become adults? More specifically, how do we become mature adults? Often, we are only aware of the labor pains as we cross over into adulthood, all the while realizing that there is no turning back. And even if this were possible, it would never be the same. It is innocence lost, and for this we often mourn. Like many, my childhood cocoon burst in such a poignantly traumatic way, spitting me out to be caught in the net of familial responsibilities.

It's New Year's Eve 1995, and I'm home nursing a painful hole in my heart. Most of my friends are in church wanting to be in the house of the Lord as the New Year ushers in. I want to be alone to think about what my family was put through this past year. I want to scream out and curse at the one who stole my grandmother and crippled my mother. It's the end of the year, and there is no one to compensate me for my year's losses. There is no one to fill the deep hole in my heart or quench the angry fires burning in my soul. So I write, hoping to exorcise my demons, cleanse my soul, and find some understanding of the God who allowed all this to happen while saying, "I love you."

My earliest memories of my grandmother are that of a tall, dark, strong-framed woman who smoked cigarettes with such intensity that the smoke blew from her nostrils like fire from a dragon's gaping jaws. Her eyes looked small behind her eyelids, but had the visual acuity to spot a silver coin on the street half a city block away. Only later as I matured did I come to appreciate the sincerity hiding behind those small eyes.

As a young boy growing up in the East Flatbush part of Brooklyn, she was my ticket to visit my older cousin Freddy, who lived on the other side of Eastern Parkway. I looked up to Freddy and enjoyed being with him. Playing with his Hot Wheels and GI Joe action figures meant the world to me. And my grandmother would be the one to take me to my little boy's nirvana. On those walking trips, she would encourage me to hurry along, as I usually was not able to keep up with her rapid pace. Returning home in the evening, I would walk next to her, stumbling along with my hands filled with borrowed toys. She in turn would slow down and move closer to me, seemingly in an effort to protect me from monsters, both real and imagined, that came out of the darkness during the long walk home. These memories now seem a lifetime away from that fateful morning when our world was irreversibly changed. It was nearly two years ago when my rest was interrupted by an unforgettable phone call.

"Pierre, your grandmother doesn't look good. She can't stop coughing, and she is complaining of pain on her left side. I don't know what to do. I've massaged her side and gave her some Tylenol, but she doesn't look good at all," my aunt said through the phone with a fear in her voice that resonated louder than her words. My father, with whom I shared an apartment on Lenox Road, in Brooklyn had awakened me. He told me that my aunt Marijo was on the phone saying that my grandmother was sick. It was one week before Christmas, 1:00 a.m. on a cold Saturday morning. Since my mother's hospitalization seven months earlier due to a stroke, my one prayer had been, "Lord, please don't let them both be sick at the same time. Let my grandmother make it through this winter."

My grandmother, Fernande Soliman, whom my family affectionately referred to as Grandfernand, had been hospitalized almost every winter for the past three years with either pneumonia or recurrent bleeding from her esophagus. She was eighty-two years old and suffered from high blood pressure along with complications of liver cirrhosis. So at the center of this dreadful nightmare I had awakened to, I advised my aunt to call an ambulance and have my grandmother taken to the hospital's medical emergency room. We lived near one another, and in the past, I would have walked the three city blocks to my grandmother's building and examine her before deciding on calling an ambulance. That morning, I was so physically and emotionally exhausted from my involvement with my mother's stroke that I was forced to leave my grandmother in God's hands.

I began to consider my relationship with my grandmother and wondered when my role in her life became that of a caretaker. It was not so long ago that she came from Haiti to live with my sister Carline, my parents, and me in a six-story apartment building in Crown Heights. My parents' marriage was filled with arguments, and they eventually separated just before I entered high school. Carline and I were raised by our mother, Sylvia, and visited our father on weekends.

During the early years when we were all together, my sister and I developed resentment toward our grandmother because she was always quick to let our mother know of all our misdeeds throughout the day. Needless to say, with our childlike logic, we considered our grandmother a spy—and consequently the cause of much of our physical punishments and frustrations.

Saturday morning was the designated day for my mother's ritualistic housecleaning, and memories recall these Saturdays as tumultuous at best. If cleanliness were next to godliness, this one-bedroom apartment would have been God's throne by every Saturday afternoon. I would be awakened by the painfully familiar sound of a broom mercilessly striking the floor. This was followed by my mother's angry voice saying to no one in particular, yet to everyone within the range of her voice, that we had better wake up, because only patients in hospitals were allowed to sleep late. One of the usual themes of her Saturday morning sermons was the condition of my grandmother's closet.

This closet was located at the right of the hallway as one entered the apartment. It seemed to contain all of her treasures in this life. To look into her closet was to catch a glimpse of her world. A tour would reveal clothes that would never be worn, letters written by old friends still in Haiti, pictures of family members, and occasionally a box of crackers meant to be opened at some special appointed time. Every Saturday morning, Grandfernand's world would be cleaned and rearranged by my mother, Sylvia. In her zeal to make all things clean, my mother would enthusiastically open the closet door and proceed to throw Grandfernand's belongings on the floor while commenting to herself, but always in earshot of Granfernand, how her closet needed to be better organized. Grandfernand, being a woman who was very comfortable with her boundaries naturally found this intrusive and disturbing, but her only vocal response was, "You know…I really don't like people harassing me." Sylvia's efforts were to be rewarded by finding the closet in the same disorganized state the following Saturday.

Going further into the house, one would enter the kitchen, where much conversation went on with Grandfernand's friends on those Saturdays when Sylvia was working. It was interesting how her friends usually came to socialize and have lunch when Sylvia was not home. Outside the kitchen window was the fire escape, which provided me with many hours of relief from New York's hot and humid summers. This was the world where Grandfernand lived for a time before moving out to live with her daughter Marijo.

When I finally arrived at the emergency room, I discovered that my grandmother was already transferred to the State University Hospital based on the recommendation of her attending physician. At the state hospital, I found her on the nursing station opposite to the one where my mother was hospitalized. At the time, I thought it pitifully ironic that I had been praying all along for this kind of situation not to come to pass, but there I was, living it. To add salt to my wound, neither of them knew that the other was just a few feet away. Of course my grandmother had known that Sylvia was hospitalized at the state hospital, but she had not visited her yet. Call it wishful thinking, but the family had hoped that Sylvia would have recovered before my grandmother was to see her. Well, things were not working out that way. Often in the past when my grandmother was hospitalized, I used to call my mother to let her know that I was keeping a close eye on Grandfernand and that she was in good hands. It gave me a wonderful feeling of satisfaction. Throughout my medical school and residency years, my mother's quiet pride in me was an emotional support beam I tightly held on to. It helped me face the emotional and psychological demands of both college and medical school. That weekend, I held on to nothing but faith and hope—faith in a God whom I believed said, "I will never leave you nor forsake you." I hoped that with divine mercy, Grandfernand would not die and Sylvia would be miraculously healed. After all, Grandfernand was hospitalized enough times in the past and lived through each one, the first occurring in 1989 at the hospital. I remember it well.

I was in the middle of my last year in medical school and living in the dormitories, luckily one block away from Grandfernand and my aunt Marijo. Sylvia had called me to say that Grandfernand was again in the emergency room and asked me to check up on her. I found Grandfernand sitting in a chair, in the crowded ER, quietly observing all the activities going on around her, with those little eyes filled with curiosity. I stood for a moment at the entrance to the ER looking at her and asked myself how she can sit there so calmly. She didn't know how to speak English, and there was no one around to translate. Marijo had a child at home to take care of and was unable to stay with her. But Grandfernand appeared remarkably calm, occasionally smiling at a doctor or nurse who met her eyes. Her English was limited to "thank you" and "you're welcome." But with those two phrases, her smile and those kind eyes, she charmed the ER staff. I reflected on how time has a way of changing one's perspective. I asked myself if this was the same person who was the cause of so much grief for Carline and me while growing up. Did she mellow out in her old age, or did I grow up?

I slowly made my way to her in the ER and greeted her, in Haitian Creole, saying, *"Grandfernand, kijan ou ye?"* (How are you?)

She responded with a wide grin, saying, *"Pierre, kisa ou ap fe isit la? Ou ta dwe ale nan klas."* (What are you doing here? You should be in class.) Followed quickly by, *"Eske ou mange deja? Ale manje lakay mwen."* (Have you eaten? Why don't you go to my house and have some food.)

I reassured her that I was eating well and came to find out how she was. I was later informed that she had pneumonia and needed to be hospitalized for treatment. I sat next to her for a while, keeping her company and answering as many questions as I could about what was going on with the other patients around her. She seemed to approach her illness not with the expected sick role but as an adventure, an opportunity to meet people and explore. Her eyes scanned the emergency room with the curiosity of a child. When she did focus on herself, her only question was, "What are they going to do with me?" Unfortunately, she spent several days and nights in the ER waiting for a hospital bed. She sat in a chair for those two days, waiting for an available stretcher, never complaining. I would see her in between my classes, and she would always ask me, *"Eske ou mange deja?"*

⸺◦◦◦◦⸺

These memories ran through my mind as I entered my grandmother's room. I was struck by the picture of her lying in bed, appearing very uncomfortable, complaining about an ache on her left side. She appeared so much smaller compared to the strong-limbed woman I knew as a little boy who used to take me out for walks. She was clearly trying to breathe in between gasps of pain as she said in Creole, "Oh, Pierre, I'm in so much pain…the left side… It's always that side." For the last eight months, my grandmother was complaining of left-sided chest pains. Her medical investigation revealed a healed left-side lower-rib fracture as the source of the pain. She was taking Tylenol tablets episodically that seemed to help for too short a time.

Before entering her room, I vowed that I would not become medically involved in her care, not ask for results of labs, and not be a doctor. I would only be a concerned grandson. Soon after entering her room, I immediately broke that vow. I found myself walking out to have the resident paged and asking for the results of various blood tests. I later regretted asking for results when I saw what they were. The results showed that she was worse off than what I thought. She was fighting for her life, and there was not a whole lot I could do about it. But I wanted to do something, anything to save her life. She was my grandmother, and I desperately needed her alive. Eventually, my emotions overwhelmed me. I was thinking as if I was her physician. To preserve my sanity, I decided to trust God even more and believe that his perfect will would be done without my interference.

I reentered the room and tried to comfort Grandfernand with my words while the resident discussed with the attending physician the best course of action to take. A little while later Claude, my mother's companion for many years, entered the room, allowing me to share this difficult moment. During times of emotional difficulties, Claude would often ease the anxiety of a situation by just being there. He continues to be there even now. Realizing that Claude was in the room, Grandfernand glanced at him and surprisingly managed to produce a smile. She went on to ask him how he was and asked me about various family members. Before we left the room and headed toward the elevator, she thankfully fell asleep, drowning out our footsteps with the sound of her snores. While waiting for the elevator, in the vacuum of silence that was now my mind, I stepped back in time to recall one weekend during my second year as a medical resident when Grandfernand had been hospitalized.

It was a free weekend long awaited for when I was not on call, and I planned to spend a day in Philadelphia with my girlfriend. I went to bed the night before filled with anticipation about the beautiful day ahead of me. Unfortunately, the night was a restless one involving a terrifying dream having to do with my grandmother in the hospital. I couldn't remember the content of the dream, but it left me with a bad feeling when I woke up. It was at least six weeks since she was hospitalized for pneumonia. It seemed to have been treated adequately by her medical team, only to return as a constantly changing chest X-ray and occasional fever. After the appropriate tests were carried out, it was discovered that she had an infection in her heart that kept seeding her lungs. She needed another month of antibiotics, at the very least.

Grandfernand was consequently transferred from the Acute Care Service to the Progressive Care Service after being declared medically stable. My visits to her became less frequent. Feeling confident that she was getting better, I made preparations to go. Getting into my car, I considered checking on Grandfernand before I left. I knew she was better but decided to check on her anyway in light of my ominous dream. I planned this to be a quick visit just to say hello.

When I walked into her room, I was shocked by the sight of Grandfernand sitting up in her hospital bed with a nasogastric tube coming out from her left nostril. I was looking at my grandmother, who was well only a few days ago, now sitting up and appearing confused.

I calmly approached her and asked what was going on. There were no other medical personnel in the room with her, which gave me a sense of surrealism as if I was in a *Twilight Zone* episode. My grandmother mentioned something about having gone to the bathroom to move her bowels earlier that morning, but somehow, I refused to make the obvious connection between her statements and the nasogastric tube. Walking out of her room, I found a nurse standing at the nurse's station. "Excuse me, nurse…what's going on with Ms. Soliman?" I asked.

Interrupting her work, she answered, "Oh, Dr. Arty, your grandmother went to the bathroom early this morning and moved some dark stools. Later on, she regurgitated some coffee-colored vomitus."

I could not understand how it was that my grandmother, or any patient for that matter, who may be having an intestinal bleed and needed the placement of a tube could be left alone. Furthermore, I soon found out that the doctor on call was on the other ward, and it was unclear when my grandmother's vitals were last taken. I knew that I had no time to express my anger or frustration toward anyone. My main concern was getting my grandmother transferred to the ICU. Eventually, the nursing staff came to assist me, but I felt as if everyone was moving in slow motion. After finding the resident on the other ward, all he could tell me with an apologetic voice was that "the patient" (my grandmother) needed to be in the ICU and he was going to discuss this with his attending.

While the resident was contacting the attending, I quickly contacted the medical senior assigned to the ICU. On the phone, I explained the situation with my grandmother and asked if there were any ICU beds available. She must have detected the urgency in my voice, because she immediately replied, "Dr. Arty, I've got one very medically stable patient occupying a bed...I'll get the intern to transfer the patient to a medical team on the floor, and you can have your grandmother prepared for transfer to the unit." A nurse quickly helped me in getting Grandfernand out of her bed onto a stretcher to facilitate transfer to the ICU. After her transfer, appropriate labs were drawn and an EKG was done, she appeared very uncomfortable in her bed—restless and jittery. She wouldn't tell me what the problem was, so I did my own investigation. What I found was a thick roll of dollar bills hidden under the covers that she had somehow kept with her without the knowledge of the medical staff. Grandfernand and I laughed out loud when I discovered the roll of bills, and ever since that time, she never stopped asking me what happened to her money. I understood without her telling me that she wanted me to have the money. But she also took joy in teasing me about how I took her money during her time of physical weakness. Oh, how many jokes we shared between us that day.

The elevator finally reached the hospital lobby and brought me back to my present circumstances. I parted with Claude and headed toward my car. I drove to a friend's house to share my thoughts and to pray. When the coping gets tough, I've often found that the best position to be in is on my knees. My respite was interrupted an hour later when I received a call from the hospital. Even as my beeper buzzed, I had a bad feeling in the pit of my stomach. It was if my insides were being tied into a knot. "Pierre," the attending said as I answered the call, "your grandmother took a turn for the worse, and I would like to know how aggressive you would like me to be with her care."

"Do everything possible for her, and I'll be right over," I quickly replied. As I was driving back to the hospital, tears began to pour down my cheeks like water from a cracked dam. I kept on wondering what God was up to.

I parked the car on Lenox Road and ran up the now familiar flight of stairs leading to the University Hospital doors. With each step, I couldn't help but think of how many times in the past I had gone this route for my grandmother, but somehow, I felt that this would be the last time. By the time I arrived onto the nursing station, my grandmother was about to be intubated and prepared for transfer to the intensive care unit. I heard her last words before being intubated. They were the words of a delirious woman calling out to family members not present in the room. She pierced the darkness of her confusion once with the words "ran swen ka manman ou" (look after your mother). She never again regained her right mind. I don't know if that was an act of mercy or a cruel joke. I prefer to think it was the former.

After her intubation, I assisted the medical staff in the transfer to the ICU where she was placed on a ventilator machine. As I saw my grandmother connected to this machine, my mind took me back to five months ago when my mother was in the same ICU on a ventilator. I guess the same thing was on the minds of the nurses, because more than one asked, "Dr. Arty, wasn't your mother here a couple of months ago? What's happened to your family?" I had no answer. What words could I put together to adequately describe the fear beating within my chest? I felt that my family was a pawn in a senseless game played by powerful unseen forces whose sole purpose was to inflict pain, and the whole world was the audience. I stood there quietly in the ICU, engaging in an unseen battle whose outcome would bring unshakable faith or turn me away from God forever.

I stayed with my grandmother in the ICU until the early hours of the morning. I felt so emotionally and physically drained that morning. Still, I trusted and prayed to the God of the universe to come through for me. I told God that I would go out and shout to the world that "Yes, God is alive and still performing miracles." He could take all the glory; I just wanted my life back. I wanted it back to how it was when I used to come home, sit in the living room either reading or watching television while my mother prepared a meal. Or I would come home before she did and prepare a surprise meal for her. Since my mother knew that I didn't know much about cooking, it gave us both a thrill when I would set the table for her and have a simple dinner ready. I wanted it back to how it was when I used to visit my grandmother on Sundays and tried to convince her to go out to either church or the park with me…when she used to give me rolls of pennies and crumpled dollar bills in a dirty handkerchief while saying, "You're going to miss me when I'm not around," and *"Bondye bon"* (God is good).

<hr />

As Sunday arrived, my girlfriend accompanied me to church service. At the end of the service, I asked the pastor to pray for my family and myself. I felt as if I had no more strength and needed new legs to hold me up. After leaving the church, we made plans to visit the hospital, finding new strength in the pastor's encouraging words. A half hour after those words, I received a page while driving to the hospital. Even before I answered I knew that it was not good news. Surprisingly, I didn't feel anxious, and there was no dread in my heart. I wish I could write that I was filled with spiritual insight and confident that even though I was walking through a very dark valley, I feared no evil. But it wasn't like that. I felt that I did all I could within my power for so long that I could do no more. Now I was going to see what God had to say. I didn't think that I was going to like it, but as long as he was saying it, I was comforted believing that my family was not a victim of purposeless circumstances.

I parked the car and went to find a phone to answer the page. We didn't carry cell phones back then, or at least I didn't. "Pierre, your grandmother is not improving. She's on maximum doses of medications, and her blood pressure is very low," the ICU attending said. Ten seconds of silence.

"Did she ever regain consciousness?" I asked, already knowing the answer.

"No," was the response.

"I should be there in twenty minutes," I said. There was no need for him to say more. Without saying it, his well-selected words told me my worst fear was about to become my reality. I thought about this as I hung up the phone and returned to my car, feeling as if I was in a daze.

As I entered the hospital ICU, I saw a woman who looked like my grandmother in the same ICU bed that I had helped to place her in several hours ago. My girlfriend thoughtfully went to speak to some of the nursing staff, leaving me to spend time alone with my grandmother. Approaching her bed, I could see that she was grotesquely swollen with the tube for breathing coming out of her mouth and connecting with plastic hoses leading to the ventilator. Her lips were swollen, and the tube was taped tightly around them. Her eyelids were slightly open so that I could see her glazed and empty stare. Her hair, wavy with curls, formed a staircase from her brow to the top of her head. It was nicely combed into two short braids. I greeted the nurses as I neared her bed. My heart had already told me who this body was while my mind maintained its silence. I touched her left arm, enjoying the warmth emanating from her being, reaching out to me and soothing me like countless times before. I gently stroked her hand and held it, enjoying the familiar coarseness of her skin. I closed her hand in mine while bending down to whisper in Creole, "Grandfernand, it's me, Pierre. Don't worry about anything. I will look after Sylvia. Remember what you've always told me, 'Bondye bon' (God is good)." I don't know if she heard me or not. Her face seemed to move toward the direction of my voice. Nonetheless, I had to say these words, to let her know that she could go in peace.

After an unclear period of time, I turned to meet the ICU attending standing by the nurses' station across from my grandmother's bed. "Hi, Pierre. I'm sorry about what's happening, but according to the labs, she's becoming very toxic, and that's affecting her blood pressure. In addition, she is anemic, and we had to transfuse a couple of units of blood. Due to her condition, we can't take a chance in moving her to get a CAT scan," he said with some hesitation. "Pierre, we're doing all we can for her." I heard the concern in his voice, in his hesitant speech and in the way he met my eyes. We both knew that the end was near.

I turned to look at my grandmother once again. She was eighty-two years old and had such a full life, raising three daughters along with several grandchildren. Many times we cheated death when the Reaper threatened to place his icy hands upon her shoulders. Together, we went through several invasive procedures. My mother would trust me to make any medical decision pertaining to my grandmother. Of course, I would discuss every aspect of her mother's care with her. In doing that, it made me feel that someone else was carrying the responsibility with me. It made my burden more than tolerable. It was an opportunity to express my love for my family. But at that moment, I felt very much alone. I wanted to go upstairs to my mother's room and ask her for guidance. But my mouth opened, and my voice quietly asked, "Lord, what do you want me to do?"

I walked slowly toward my grandmother's bed and didn't know how to say good-bye. I didn't know how to tell her that I was going to let her go…that rather than fighting death as we had often done in the past we've finally lost the war. I watched as her eyes continued to stare into space and listened to the sound of the ventilator helping her breathe. I looked at the tubes and intravenous lines invading her body. Her bloated lifeless form all seemed to mock the life she lived.

I placed her left hand in mine once again, holding it tightly with both hands as if trying to pull her back to me, to prevent her spirit from leaving. I bent down to kiss her hands, feeling the dryness of her skin with my lips, trying to capture her presence with all of my senses. Once again, I leaned toward her ear, wanting to say good-bye but could not. I couldn't even think it. In my mind, I silently said, "I love you." I straightened up, wiped the tears from my eyes, and walked back to the ICU attending. "Listen," I said with a cracked voice, "I know that you're doing all that you can for her…I want you to let her go in peace…on her own. She's been through enough. What I'm telling you is that if her heart should stop…don't try to bring her back."

"I understand," he responded. I went on to sign the necessary do-not-resuscitate papers required to finalize my decision. As I signed the form, I wondered if I was doing the right thing. I wondered if my mother would agree or understand how I came to sign these papers. Afterward, I called my sister and aunt, letting them know what I decided and why.

They didn't object. I then went upstairs to my mother's room and sat on the visitor's chair next to her bed. She was sleeping, oblivious to the madness I just went through, seeming so calm and restful. I stayed there sitting next to her, wanting her to reach out and hold me with her words as she had done so many times in the past.

Tonight, it's New Year's Eve, and I want to tally up my gains and losses. I don't want to waste the tears already shed, so I write, hoping to ease the ache in my soul and make peace with my God. Suddenly, I raise my voice, breaking the silence of my room, and ask, "Where were you in all this? Why did you let this happen?" I'm very much tempted to think that the creator of heaven and earth was on some celestial vacation when all this insanity chose my family to express itself. But like a soothing balm, my grandmother's words, *"Bondye bon,"* comes to my mind's ear. For me, those two simple words contain the key to resolving the turmoil in my soul and my anchor to sanity. She didn't have a formal education. As I think about her, I can't recall my grandmother ever reading anything, secular or religious. But she was no fool. She learned the most difficult lesson in life, which is to trust in the goodness and sovereignty of God always. She literally lived her faith. Her belief was simple, alive…not simply cerebral. It was laced into every fragment of her being.

Like Job, she never cursed God but maintained her testimony, blindly trusting in her God even when the answers never came. I heard those simple words when her eldest daughter died from a stroke. I heard them when my mother lay comatose in an ICU bed for almost three weeks, and no one knew whether she would live or die. For me, there were times I became so angry that I would shut my eyes, make a fist as if to fight the invisible culprit who did all this to us, and force this malevolence to make it all right again, only to open my eyes and see my mother's crippled form knowing that I was powerless to heal her. If someone had told me that God had it in for me, that he hated me, I wouldn't believe it. But I would think it plausible in light of my circumstances.

I continue to hold on to my grandmother's words like beacons, guiding me through this life of uncertainties and contradictions. I don't know if she ever asked the question I find myself asking. Needless to say, the answers to my prayers were not what I had envisioned. But in believing simply that *"Bondye bon,"* it pushes me to have faith like my grandmother in the goodness of God. It pushes me further to believe that even in my grandmother's death and my mother's incapacity, somehow God does have my best interest at heart. It takes a moment to write this but a lifetime to live it—and maybe even longer to believe it.

Tonight, I thank God for the little things: my mother's beautiful smile when I tell her a joke, her look of wonder when I share my plans with her, the expression of joy on her face when I say to her, "I love you," and the way she carefully adjusts my coat collar with her left hand before I leave her hospital room. Occasionally, I dream about the way things were. Sometimes the dreams are so intense that when I wake up, I desperately try to hold on to the midst of my dreams, to continue savoring the quickly fading memory of what was once upon a time.

So I continue to write, expelling my demons with each stroke of my pen. I expose my heart, hoping to find healing and once again embrace the God who encourages me to boast in my knowledge of Him. This is my story and maybe in some ways is yours also. It is a timeless and familiar story, of a search for meaning in the midst of pain, loss, and disappointment. I continue to *"ran swen ka manman mwen"* (look after my mother), whose body is now a painful memory of the woman I once knew—all the while living with uncertainties and believing that God is good.

About the Author

Pierre Richard Arty, M.D. was born in Cap-Haitien, Haiti, and raised in the East Flatbush section of Brooklyn, New York. He is an enthusiastic and creative writer who is sought-after to provide education about mental illness to the medical as well as faith-based community.

Dr. Arty attended Columbia College of Columbia University, where he completed a premedical concentration in political science. He graduated from SUNY Downstate Medical School in Brooklyn in 1990. After completing an Internal Medicine Residency at Kings County Hospital, in Brooklyn, New York, he pursued a Fellowship in Addictive Medicine, followed by a residency in Psychiatry at the same institution. He is board-certified in psychiatry and Addiction Medicine.

Dr. Arty serves as an Elder at Abounding Grace Ministries on New York City's Lower East Side. He is the overseer of the Drama Ministry. He is also an active member of the medical missions team at The Brooklyn Tabernacle and travels to other nations to provide medical and spiritual care to the underserved. He is a board member of World Compassion Fellowship. He is also a board member of the SUNY Downstate Medical College Alumni Association and Diaspora Community Services.

Dr. Arty works in New York City and lives in Brooklyn, New York.

CPSIA information can be obtained
at www.ICGtesting.com
Printed in the USA
BVOW03s0733281117
501377BV00023B/113/P